AN INTRODUCTION TO
PROGRAM EVALUATION

BASIC CONCEPTS AND EXAMPLE CASES

Printed in the United States of America
Lightning Source (Ingram) Books, Inc. (US)
1246 Heil Quaker Blvd.
La Vergne, TN 37086
USA

Printed in the United Kingdom
Lightning Source (Ingram) Books UK Ltd.
Chapter House
Pitfield
Kiln Farm
Milton Keynes MK 11 3LW
UK

Printed in Australia
Lightning Source (Ingram) Books AU Pty Ltd.
Unit A 1/A3
7 Janine Street
Scoresby, Victoria 3179
Australia

Cover, Design, Page Layout and Composition
Lidija Markovic

Canadian Cataloguing in Publication Data
Jones, Richard Merrick, 1947-

An Introduction to Program Evaluation:
Basic Concepts and Example Cases

ISBN: 978-0-9684857-4-3

1. Program 2. Evaluation 3. Program Evaluation
4. Evaluation Research (Social Action Programs)
5. Jones, Richard Merrick

RICHARD M. JONES

AN INTRODUCTION TO
PROGRAM
EVALUATION

BASIC CONCEPTS AND EXAMPLE CASES

CONTENTS

EXAMPLE CASES

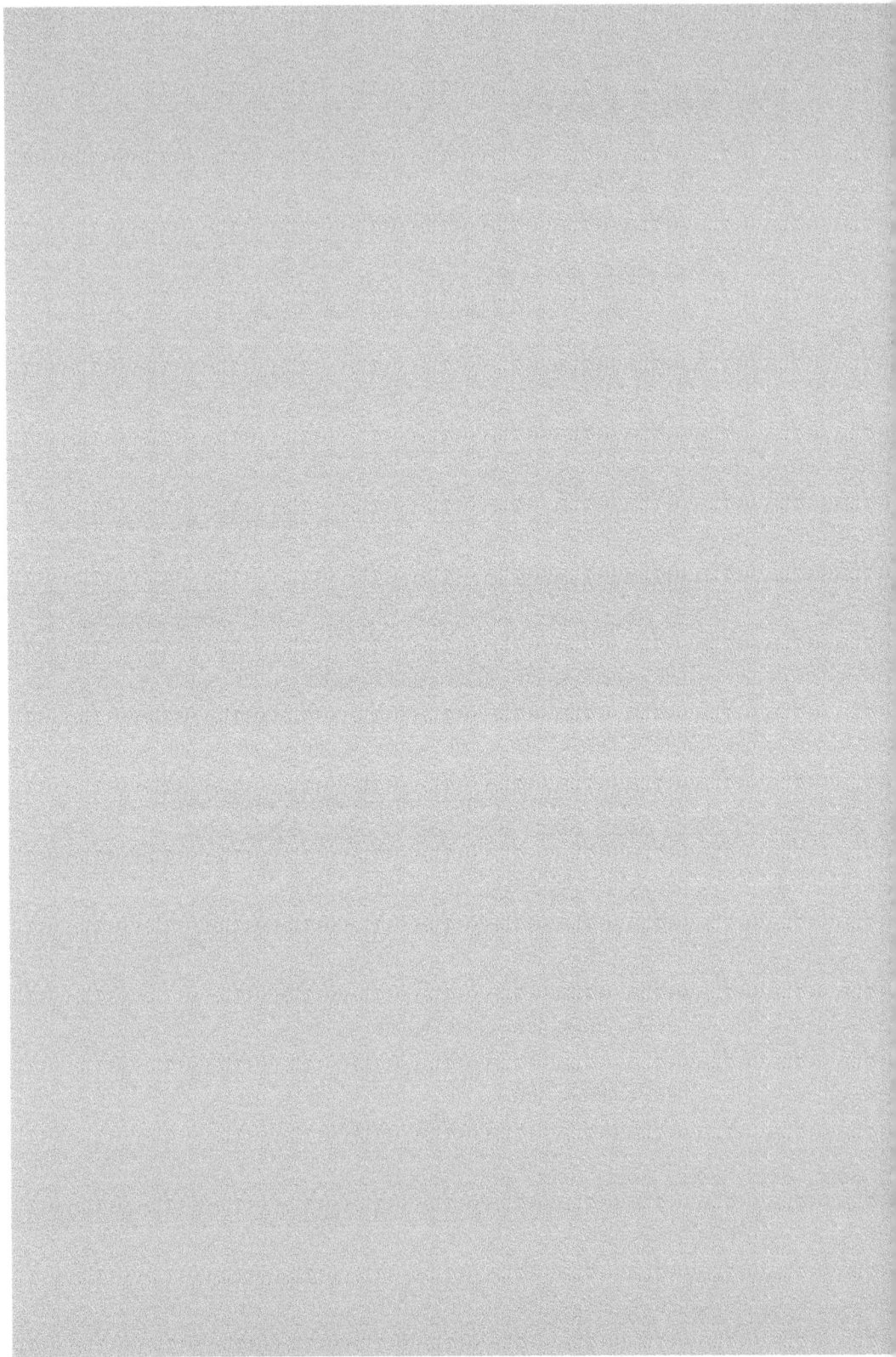

ABOUT THE AUTHOR

Richard Jones has worked in the field of evaluation for more than three decades. Currently, he is Director of Assessment with the Education Quality and Accountability Office (EQAO) in Toronto. Prior to this, Dr. Jones was Project Manager for National, International and Special Projects with EQAO; Director of Assessment and Evaluation with the Saskatchewan Department of Education and Coordinator of Provincial Learning Assessment and Assistant Director of the Provincial and Scholarship Examination Program with the British Columbia Ministry of Education. In these various roles his responsibilities have included designing and implementing initiatives related to student evaluation, program evaluation, curriculum evaluation, provincial learning assessment, education quality indicators, school and school board improvement planning and accreditation, as well as national and international assessments.

Dr. Jones taught for many years at the elementary, secondary, community college and university levels in Ontario, British Columbia and South Africa. He served as researcher and senior manager for an American-based consulting firm on program evaluation projects in the Middle East. He has consulted, made presentations at conferences and provided in-service workshops on assessment and evaluation for professional organizations in Asia, Europe, the Middle East and North America. He has authored several journal articles, as well as book chapters and books on assessment and evaluation topics. Over the years, Dr. Jones has conducted numerous program evaluation studies in both the public and private sectors in Canada and abroad.

ACKNOWLEDGEMENTS

I wish to acknowledge and thank the following organizations that granted me permission to reference information and/or describe program evaluation methodologies with the understanding that the studies' findings, recommendations and identifying information about personnel would not be included in this publication:

- Economics Research Associates (at the time of the studies a subsidiary of Planning Research Corporation) for permission to describe the methodologies of the evaluation projects conducted in the Kingdom of Saudi Arabia

- Insurance Institute of Canada for permission to describe the methods used in a program evaluation project conducted for the Institute

- Saskatchewan Ministry of Education for permission to use content from the document *Saskatchewan School-Based Program Evaluation Resource Book (1989)* and refer to methodology used in program evaluation studies conducted for the Ministry[1]

I am grateful to the Joint Committee on Standards for Educational Evaluation and the American Evaluation Association for granting me permission to include *The Program Evaluation Standards* and the *Guiding Principles for Evaluators,* respectively, in this resource.

---

[1] Over the years, Saskatchewan Education has introduced a number of excellent, innovative programs. In the 1980s, the Ministry commissioned the writing of the *Saskatchewan School-Based Program Evaluation Resource Book* and accompanying workshop series. This was done in recognition of the importance of program evaluation as a professional activity to enhance decision making and program change, not just in education but in any field of endeavor. I have used the Saskatchewan resource book as my first reference when conducting program evaluation projects, and it has been a valuable source of information in preparing this publication.

Thanks are due all of my colleagues who participated with me on program evaluation studies over the years. In particular, I wish to acknowledge the following people:

- Evelyn Mazurkie, former Education Consultant, Senior Program Manager and Assistant Registrar, Saskatchewan Education: Program Evaluation of the Indian and Métis Education Staff Development Program
- Catherine Sim, former Education Officer, Education Quality and Accountability Office (EQAO) and current Manager, 21st Century Learning, Ontario Ministry of Education: Scenic Valley School Division Evaluation of the Program for Protected Classroom Instruction (PPCI) and the Examinations Study for the Insurance Institute of Canada
- Gilberte Spooner, former Education Officer, EQAO: Evaluation of the Ontario Academic Course Teacher In-service Program

I would also like to express my appreciation to Dr. H. Jon Dada, Ph.D., a colleague in conducting the Study to Establish Social Institutions in Saudi Arabia, for his support in describing the study's methodology.

A special note of thanks is extended to Lidija Markovic for her expertise in cover design, page layout and composition. Her professionalism and creativity were instrumental in the creation of this book.

INTRODUCTION

PURPOSE AND AUDIENCES

Program evaluation, if conducted appropriately, has the potential to provide information that helps decision makers

- make informed decisions about the extent to which programs or aspects of programs are working as intended;
- effect changes to existing programs to make them more effective and
- implement (or decide whether or not to implement) new programs/initiatives, procedures or products.

Access to valid, accurate data/information, therefore, is critical to those who have responsibility for making decisions.

As part of an organization, you may be interested in conducting an "internal" program evaluation, or you may wish to engage an evaluation consultant to conduct an "external" program evaluation. In any case, it is important to understand the basics of program evaluation in order to design and conduct a successful study or to be an educated client/consumer. Over the years, many articles and books have been written on the multitude of approaches to conducting program evaluation; however, the truth is that the basic technology of evaluation (the principles and procedures) has not changed to any great degree. In addition, many of the available resources are written in technical language. The purpose of this resource, therefore, is to provide a plain-language resource for students of introductory post-secondary courses on program evaluation, those who are relative novices in evaluation who wish to conduct or commission program evaluation work and stakeholders of program evaluation studies.

ORGANIZATION OF THE BOOK

Chapters 1 to 4 of this resource present introductory background information about program evaluation. Chapter 1 provides information about selected basic concepts. Underlying all program evaluation activities are standards of best practice and ethical issues which must be considered at the outset and attended to throughout a program evaluation study; Chapter 2 is dedicated to these standards and ethical principles. A brief overview of various approaches to conducting program evaluation and a six-step, basic program evaluation process are presented in Chapters 3 and 4, respectively.

Over the years, I have delivered workshops and courses in program evaluation and have conducted program evaluation projects in both the public and private sectors in Canada and abroad. Chapters 5 to

14 provide example cases of program evaluation projects in which I have participated. These cases provide a variety of real-life evaluation methodologies to demonstrate how the fundamental standards of practice and ethical issues were considered and applied in designing and conducting the program evaluation studies.

Program evaluation is my first love in the field of evaluation. I believe it is the combination of science (the application of rigorous principles and methods) and art (the judgement and creative problem-solving aspects, particularly in study design) that I find so appealing. I hope that you will find this book to be a useful introductory resource whether you personally conduct program evaluation projects or simply wish to be a more informed client/consumer.

BASIC CONCEPTS

BASIC CONCEPTS IN PROGRAM EVALUATION

INTRODUCTION

Information about the following basic concepts is provided as an introduction to the topic of program evaluation:

- Definition of Program Evaluation
- Purpose(s) of Program Evaluation
- Informal and Formal Evaluation
- Formative and Summative Evaluation
- Internal and External Evaluation
- Potential Value and Limitations of Evaluation

DEFINITION OF PROGRAM EVALUATION

The following definition of program evaluation (Yarbrough, Shulha, Hopson & Caruthers, 2011) is used for the purposes of this resource:

> - the systematic investigation of the quality of programs, projects, subprograms, subprojects, and/or any of their components or elements, together or singly
> - for the purposes of decision making, judgments, conclusions, findings, new knowledge, organizational development, and capacity building in response to the needs of identified stakeholders
> - leading to improvement and/or accountability in the users' programs and systems
> - ultimately contributing to organizational or social value. (p. xxv)

As the definition suggests, when a program evaluation is undertaken, it may focus on an entire program (e.g., the Ontario Ministry of Health's Ontario Health Insurance Plan [OHIP]) or one or more aspects of a program (e.g., OHIP's application process). The following list of potential focuses of program evaluation is adapted from Saskatchewan Education (1989):

- Products/initiatives/services (the result(s) being achieved or desired; assessment of need or feasibility)
- Procedures/Processes/Approaches (how things operate, or how they are/might be done)
- Resources (the human and/or material resources which are/ might be available and are being/might be utilized)

- Clients/stakeholders (how they are/might be involved with or related to the program or aspect of the program under consideration)
- Staff/Personnel (how they are/might be involved with or relate to the program or aspect of the program under consideration)

Program evaluation, for the purposes of this resource, is used in the broadest possible context and corresponds with the position of McNamara (2008a) who states that

> Program evaluation can include any or a variety of at least 35 different types of evaluation, such as for needs assessments, accreditation, cost/benefit analysis, effectiveness, efficiency, formative, summative, goal-based, process, outcomes, etc. (p. 3)

This wide-ranging view of program evaluation is supported by numerous authors including Hudson, Mayne and Thomlison (1992); Love (1991); Saskatchewan Education (1989); Stufflebeam and Coryn (2014) and Worthen, Sanders and Fitzpatrick (1997).

PURPOSE(S) OF PROGRAM EVALUATION

Hearing the word "evaluation," many people think that the purpose of program evaluation is to determine whether or not an organization or a program is successful. The result is that often those who have program responsibility feel threatened by the prospect of evaluation. It is important, however, to realize that in the real world there is no such thing as a perfect program; there is always room for improvement. Being open to feedback and continuing to make adjustments where necessary will go a long way toward ensuring the success of a program and/or an organization.

Hudson, et al. (1992) identify four general purposes of program evaluation:

- Increase knowledge (to increase our knowledge and understanding about an intervention in society)
- Improve program delivery (to improve the management and delivery of a program)
- Reconsider program direction (to challenge the strategic direction of a program)
- Provide for accountability (to provide performance information for accountability)

INFORMAL AND FORMAL EVALUATION

Program evaluation can be either informal or formal.

According to Worthen, et al. (1997), informal evaluation takes place where

> **66** ...choices are based on highly subjective perceptions of which alternative is best.... **99**

Formal evaluation takes place where

> **66** choices are based on systematic efforts to define explicit criteria and obtain accurate information about alternatives.... (p. 7) **99**

The decision by a municipal council to rezone a tract of land without reference to community and environmental impact studies might serve as an example of an informal evaluation.

FORMATIVE AND SUMMATIVE EVALUATION

Evaluation can be either formative or summative. Formative evaluation is conducted to obtain information for program improvement; whereas, summative evaluation is conducted in order to make judgements about a program's success or merit.

INTERNAL AND EXTERNAL EVALUATION

Worthen, et al. (1997) differentiate internal and external evaluation in the following way: Internal evaluations are those that are conducted by employees internal to the organization. External evaluations are those that are conducted by consultants from outside the organization. This distinction becomes muddied when (for example) evaluators come from another branch of the same organization. From the perspective of the staff associated with the program under review, the program evaluation might be considered external. From the perspective of senior management of the organization, the program evaluation might be considered internal. The authors state that often formative evaluations are conducted internally to involve personnel with direct program knowledge, and because the lack of objectivity is not as problematic as it would be with summative evaluation. Summative evaluations, on the other hand, are most often conducted by external evaluators.

POTENTIAL VALUE AND LIMITATIONS OF EVALUATION

Program evaluation, if well executed, has the potential to provide information that will help decision makers make informed choices that could lead to new or more effective programs, procedures or products. Evaluation, however, does not solve problems: people do. As Worthen, et al. (1997) contend:

> **"** Though evaluation can be enormously useful, it is generally counterproductive for evaluators or those who depend on their work to propose evaluation as the ultimate solution to every problem or, indeed, as any sort of solution, because evaluation in and of itself won't affect a solution–though it may suggest one. Evaluation serves to identify strengths and weaknesses, highlight the good, and expose the faulty, but it cannot singlehandedly correct problems, for that is the role of management and other stakeholders, using evaluation findings as one tool that will help them in that process. Evaluation has a role to play in enlightening its consumers, and it may be used for many other roles. But it is only one of many influences on improving the policies, practices, and decisions in the institutions that are important to us. (p. 23) **"**

SUMMARY

A program may be viewed as any type of system which initiates action(s) toward achieving some goal(s). Formal program evaluation involves the systematic examination of a program or one or more of its components for a multitude of purposes, including knowledge acquisition, accountability and decision making with regard to initiating new directions/programs and effecting program improvement or change. Program evaluation may be formal or informal, formative or summative and may be conducted internally by those within an organization or externally by outside expert consultants. In and of itself, program evaluation is not the be-all and end-all; it does not provide the ultimate solution(s). The outcome(s) of well-executed evaluation can provide valuable information with which to make informed decisions and suggest direction for action.

STANDARDS OF PRACTICE AND ETHICAL CONSIDERATIONS

2

INTRODUCTION

Since the mid-1970s, increased attention has been paid to standards of practice and ethical issues in evaluation. Two professional organizations in the United States, the Joint Committee on Standards for Educational Evaluation (2011) and the American Evaluation Association (2004), have published *The Program Evaluation Standards* and *Guiding Principles for Evaluators,* respectively. Although there is some overlap between the *Standards* and *Principles* documents, the *Standards'* primary focus is on standards of practice (or the soundness of the evaluation design and methodology); whereas, the *Principles'* primary focus is on professional ethics.

Whenever tests form part of program evaluation, it is important to ensure they are well-constructed, can provide for useful interpretation and are valid for their intended purposes. Two valuable resources, *Standards for Educational and Psychological Testing* (2014) and *Principles for Fair Student Assessment Practices for Education in Canada* (1993), provide fundamental standards and principles for testing practices.

Both practitioners who conduct program evaluation and clients and/or stakeholders of program evaluation studies need to be well informed about associated ethical issues, as well as standards of practice. Worthen, et al. (1997) state that

> Important as methodological and technical expertise are to good evaluation, that importance is often overshadowed by the interpersonal, ethical, and political influences that shape the evaluator's work. Many a good evaluation, unimpeachable in all technical details, has failed because of interpersonal insensitivity, ethical compromises, or political naiveté. (p. 311)

Guiding program evaluation standards of practice and ethical principles are presented below.

THE PROGRAM EVALUATION STANDARDS

Standards of practice are key underpinnings of any professional endeavor and are essential in conducting program evaluation. Stufflebeam and Coryn (2014) state the following:

> Professional standards for guiding and judging evaluations are essential to the sound practice of evaluation. Such standards help ensure that evaluators and their clients communicate effectively and reach a clear, mutual understanding concerning the criteria an evaluation should meet, and they provide authoritative guidance for meeting the criteria. Professional standards also help prevent the possibility that either stakeholders or evaluators might unscrupulously bend evaluation outcomes to suit their own interests. (p. 69)

The program evaluation standards statements, produced by the Joint Committee on Standards for Educational Evaluation (2011), are presented below. Evaluators and evaluation users are encouraged to read the complete book (Yarbrough, Shulha, Hopson, & Caruthers, 2011) to gain a thorough understanding of the standards.

UTILITY STANDARDS

The utility standards are intended to increase the extent to which program stakeholders find evaluation processes and products valuable in meeting their needs.

U1 Evaluator Credibility

Evaluations should be conducted by qualified people who establish and maintain credibility in the evaluation context.

U2 Attention to Stakeholders

Evaluations should devote attention to the full range of individuals and groups invested in the program and affected by its evaluation.

U3 Negotiated Purposes

Evaluation purposes should be identified and continually negotiated based on the needs of stakeholders.

U4 Explicit Values

Evaluations should clarify and specify the individual and cultural values underpinning purposes, processes, and judgments.

U5 Relevant Information

Evaluation information should serve the identified and emergent needs of stakeholders.

U6 Meaningful Processes and Products

Evaluations should construct activities, descriptions, and judgments in ways that encourage participants to rediscover, reinterpret, or revise their understandings and behaviors.

UTILITY STANDARDS (CONTINUED)

U7 Timely and Appropriate Communicating and Reporting

Evaluations should attend to the continuing information needs of their multiple audiences.

U8 Concern for Consequences and Influence

Evaluations should promote responsible and adaptive use while guarding against unintended negative consequences and misuse.

FEASIBILITY STANDARDS

The feasibility standards are intended to increase evaluation effectiveness and efficiency.

F1 Project Management

Evaluations should use effective project management strategies.

F2 Practical Procedures

Evaluation procedures should be practical and responsive to the way the program operates.

F3 Contextual Viability

Evaluations should recognize, monitor, and balance the cultural and political interests and needs of individuals and groups.

F4 Resource Use

Evaluations should use resources effectively and efficiently.

PROPRIETY STANDARDS

The propriety standards support what is proper, fair, legal, right and just in evaluations.

P1 Responsive and Inclusive Orientation

Evaluations should be responsive to stakeholders and their communities.

P2 Formal Agreements

Evaluation agreements should be negotiated to make obligations explicit and take into account the needs, expectations, and cultural contexts of clients and other stakeholders.

P3 Human Rights and Respect

Evaluations should be designed and conducted to protect human and legal rights and maintain the dignity of participants and other stakeholders.

P4 Clarity and Fairness

Evaluations should be understandable and fair in addressing stakeholder needs and purposes.

P5 Transparency and Disclosure

Evaluations should provide complete descriptions of findings, limitations, and conclusions to all stakeholders, unless doing so would violate legal and propriety obligations.

P6 Conflicts of Interests

Evaluations should openly and honestly identify and address real or perceived conflicts of interests that may compromise the evaluation.

P7 Fiscal Responsibility

Evaluations should account for all expended resources and comply with sound fiscal procedures and processes.

ACCURACY STANDARDS

The accuracy standards are intended to increase the dependability and truthfulness of evaluation representations, propositions, and findings, especially those that support interpretations and judgments about quality.

A1   Justified Conclusions and Decisions

Evaluation conclusions and decisions should be explicitly justified in the cultures and contexts where they have consequences.

A2   Valid Information

Evaluation information should serve the intended purposes and support valid interpretations.

A3   Reliable Information

Evaluation procedures should yield sufficiently dependable and consistent information for the intended uses.

A4   Explicit Program and Context Descriptions

Evaluations should document programs and their contexts with appropriate detail and scope for the evaluation purposes.

A5   Information Management

Evaluations should employ systematic information collection, review, verification, and storage methods.

A6   Sound Designs and Analyses

Evaluations should employ technically adequate designs and analyses that are appropriate for the evaluation purposes.

A7   Explicit Evaluation Reasoning

Evaluation reasoning leading from information and analyses to findings, interpretations, conclusions, and judgments should be clearly and completely documented.

A8   Communication and Reporting

Evaluation communications should have adequate scope and guard against misconceptions, biases, distortions, and errors.

EVALUATION ACCOUNTABILITY STANDARDS

The evaluation accountability standards encourage adequate documentation of evaluations and a metaevaluative perspective focused on improvement and accountability for evaluation processes and products.

E1 Evaluation Documentation

Evaluations should fully document their negotiated purposes and implemented designs, procedures, data, and outcomes.

E2 Internal Metaevaluation

Evaluators should use these and other applicable standards to examine the accountability of the evaluation design, procedures employed, information collected, and outcomes.

E3 External Metaevaluation

Program evaluation sponsors, clients, evaluators, and other stakeholders should encourage the conduct of external metaevaluations using these and other applicable standards.

GUIDING PRINCIPLES FOR EVALUATORS

Whereas the program evaluation standards focus on the concepts of utility, feasibility, propriety, accuracy and accountability in evaluation, the guiding principles for evaluators emphasize standards of professional conduct. In the words of Stufflebeam and Coryn (2014):

> **❝** The 2004 AEA guiding principles for evaluators provide evaluators with a code of professional behavior. The principles are also applicable to evaluating evaluation designs and reports across a wide array of disciplines. They encourage evaluators to practice systematic inquiry and to serve society by acting honestly and giving priority to the public welfare throughout their professional career and in conducting evaluations. (p. 83) **❞**

Following are the *Guiding Principles for Evaluators*, produced by the American Evaluation Association (2004).

A

SYSTEMATIC INQUIRY

Evaluators conduct systematic, data-based inquiries.

1 To ensure the accuracy and credibility of the evaluative information they produce, evaluators should adhere to the highest technical standards appropriate to the methods they use.

2 Evaluators should explore with the client the shortcomings and strengths both of the various evaluation questions and the various approaches that might be used for answering those questions.

3 Evaluators should communicate their methods and approaches accurately and in sufficient detail to allow others to understand, interpret and critique their work. They should make clear the limitations of an evaluation and its results. Evaluators should discuss in a contextually appropriate way those values, assumptions, theories, methods, results, and analyses significantly affecting the interpretation of the evaluative findings. These statements apply to all aspects of the evaluation, from its initial conceptualization to the eventual use of findings.

B

COMPETENCE

Evaluators provide competent performance to stakeholders.

1   Evaluators should possess (or ensure that the evaluation team possesses)
    the education, abilities, skills and experience appropriate to undertake the
    tasks proposed in the evaluation.

2   To ensure recognition, accurate interpretation and respect for diversity,
    evaluators should ensure that the members of the evaluation team
    collectively demonstrate cultural competence. Cultural competence would
    be reflected in evaluators seeking awareness of their own culturally-based
    assumptions, their understanding of the worldviews of culturally-different
    participants and stakeholders in the evaluation, and the use of appropriate
    evaluation strategies and skills in working with culturally different groups.
    Diversity may be in terms of race, ethnicity, gender, religion, socio-
    economics, or other factors pertinent to the evaluation context.

3   Evaluators should practice within the limits of their professional training
    and competence, and should decline to conduct evaluations that fall
    substantially outside those limits. When declining the commission or
    request is not feasible or appropriate, evaluators should make clear any
    significant limitations on the evaluation that might result. Evaluators should
    make every effort to gain the competence directly or through the assistance
    of others who possess the required expertise.

4   Evaluators should continually seek to maintain and improve their
    competencies, in order to provide the highest level of performance in their
    evaluations. This continuing professional development might include formal
    coursework and workshops, self-study, evaluations of one's own practice,
    and working with other evaluators to learn from their skills and expertise.

INTEGRITY/HONESTY

C

Evaluators display honesty and integrity in their own behavior, and attempt to ensure the honesty and integrity of the entire evaluation process.

1 Evaluators should negotiate honestly with clients and relevant stakeholders concerning the costs, tasks to be undertaken, limitations of methodology, scope of results likely to be obtained, and uses of data resulting from a specific evaluation. It is primarily the evaluator's responsibility to initiate discussion and clarification of these matters, not the client's.

2 Before accepting an evaluation assignment, evaluators should disclose any roles or relationships they have that might pose a conflict of interest (or appearance of a conflict) with their role as an evaluator. If they proceed with the evaluation, the conflict(s) should be clearly articulated in reports of the evaluation results.

3 Evaluators should record all changes made in the originally negotiated project plans, and the reasons why the changes were made. If those changes would significantly affect the scope and likely results of the evaluation, the evaluator should inform the client and other important stakeholders in a timely fashion (barring good reason to the contrary, before proceeding with further work) of the changes and their likely impact.

4 Evaluators should be explicit about their own, their clients', and other stakeholders' interests and values concerning the conduct and outcomes of an evaluation.

5 Evaluators should not misrepresent their procedures, data or findings. Within reasonable limits, they should attempt to prevent or correct misuse of their work by others.

6 If evaluators determine that certain procedures or activities are likely to produce misleading evaluative information or conclusions, they have the responsibility to communicate their concerns and the reasons for them. If discussions with the client do not resolve these concerns, the evaluator should decline to conduct the evaluation. If declining the assignment is unfeasible or inappropriate, the evaluator should consult colleagues or relevant stakeholders about other proper ways to proceed. (Options might include discussions at a higher level, a dissenting cover letter or appendix, or refusal to sign the final document.)

7 Evaluators should disclose all sources of financial support for an evaluation, and the source of the request for the evaluation.

RESPECT FOR PEOPLE

D

Evaluators respect the security, dignity and self-worth of respondents, program participants, clients, and other evaluation stakeholders.

1 Evaluators should seek a comprehensive understanding of the important contextual elements of the evaluation. Contextual factors that may influence the results of a study include geographic location, timing, political and social climate, economic conditions, and other relevant activities in progress at the same time.

2 Evaluators should abide by current professional ethics, standards, and regulations regarding risks, harms, and burdens that might befall those participating in the evaluation; regarding informed consent for participation in evaluation; and regarding informing participants and clients about the scope and limits of confidentiality.

3 Because justified negative or critical conclusions from an evaluation must be explicitly stated, evaluations sometimes produce results that harm client or stakeholder interests. Under this circumstance, evaluators should seek to maximize the benefits and reduce any unnecessary harms that might occur, provided this will not compromise the integrity of the evaluation findings. Evaluators should carefully judge when the benefits from doing the evaluation or in performing certain evaluation procedures should be foregone because of the risks or harms. To the extent possible, these issues should be anticipated during the negotiation of the evaluation.

4 Knowing that evaluations may negatively affect the interests of some stakeholders, evaluators should conduct the evaluation and communicate its results in a way that clearly respects the stakeholders' dignity and self-worth.

5 Where feasible, evaluators should attempt to foster social equity in evaluation, so that those who give to the evaluation may benefit in return. For example, evaluators should seek to ensure that those who bear the burdens of contributing data and incurring any risks do so willingly, and that they have full knowledge of and opportunity to obtain any benefits of the evaluation. Program participants should be informed that their eligibility to receive services does not hinge on their participation in the evaluation.

6 Evaluators have the responsibility to understand and respect differences among participants, such as differences in their culture, religion, gender, disability, age, sexual orientation and ethnicity, and to account for potential implications of these differences when planning, conducting, analyzing, and reporting evaluations.

E

RESPONSIBILITIES FOR GENERAL AND PUBLIC WELFARE

Evaluators articulate and take into account the diversity of general and public interests and values that may be related to the evaluation.

1   When planning and reporting evaluations, evaluators should include relevant perspectives and interests of the full range of stakeholders.

2   Evaluators should consider not only the immediate operations and outcomes of whatever is being evaluated, but also its broad assumptions, implications and potential side effects.

3   Freedom of information is essential in a democracy. Evaluators should allow all relevant stakeholders access to evaluative information in forms that respect people and honor promises of confidentiality. Evaluators should actively disseminate information to stakeholders as resources allow. Communications that are tailored to a given stakeholder should include all results that may bear on interests of that stakeholder and refer to any other tailored communications to other stakeholders. In all cases, evaluators should strive to present results clearly and simply so that clients and other stakeholders can easily understand the evaluation process and results.

4   Evaluators should maintain a balance between client needs and other needs. Evaluators necessarily have a special relationship with the client who funds or requests the evaluation. By virtue of that relationship, evaluators must strive to meet legitimate client needs whenever it is feasible and appropriate to do so. However, that relationship can also place evaluators in difficult dilemmas when client interests conflict with other interests, or when client interests conflict with the obligation of evaluators for systematic inquiry, competence, integrity, and respect for people. In these cases, evaluators should explicitly identify and discuss the conflicts with the client and relevant stakeholders, resolve them when possible, determine whether continued work on the evaluation is advisable if the conflicts cannot be resolved, and make clear any significant limitations on the evaluation that might result if the conflict is not resolved.

5   Evaluators have obligations that encompass the public interest and good. These obligations are especially important when evaluators are supported by publicly-generated funds; but clear threats to the public good should never be ignored in any evaluation. Because the public interest and good are rarely the same as the interests of any particular group (including those of the client or funder), evaluators will usually have to go beyond analysis of particular stakeholder interests and consider the welfare of society as a whole.

SUMMARY

Standards of best practice and ethical behaviour must be addressed if program evaluations are to be useful and worthwhile and if the interests of all those involved in or affected by program evaluations are to be safeguarded. It must be recognized that a perfect program evaluation does not exist. However, by bearing in mind the standards and principles presented in this chapter, there is greater likelihood a program evaluation study will be successful. In subsequent chapters of this book, examples are provided from program evaluation studies in which I have participated to illustrate how many of these standards and principles can be addressed.

APPROACHES TO PROGRAM EVALUATION

INTRODUCTION

Program evaluations generally follow a common series of steps or procedures, which will be described in Chapter 4. However, first it must be acknowledged that there are many approaches that can provide useful ideas for program evaluation design. This chapter will present brief descriptions of these approaches for the purpose of general awareness; example references are cited for those who wish more detailed information.

PROGRAM EVALUATION APPROACHES

Over the years, the number of evaluation approaches has proliferated, and numerous authors have provided comparative analyses of the characteristics of the various approaches and/or have devised classification schemas for them. As was mentioned earlier, more than 35 different program evaluation models/approaches have been proposed. Among these, some of the best-known approaches are described by Saskatchewan Education (1989).[2]

---

[2] The information about selected approaches is excerpted or adapted from the Saskatchewan *School-Based Program Evaluation Resource Book* (1989).

Objectives-Oriented Evaluation

Objectives-oriented evaluation approaches are those that compare results with established objectives. Three approaches are identified below.

The Basic Approach involves establishing the goals or objectives, analyzing the objectives to identify and clarify their basic dimensions, identifying how performance related to the goals or objectives will be measured, collecting performance data and comparing the data with the goals or objectives.

The Four-Question Approach involves designing an evaluation through responding to four questions: Why? (What needs can you identify that justify the existence of the program?) What? (What are the objectives of the program? What are the objectives designed to accomplish in order to meet the needs?) How? (How will the program function to meet its objectives?) How will you know? (What kinds of information should be gathered to find out if the How is meeting the What for the Why?)

The Goal-Free Approach is one in which the evaluator deliberately ignores the objectives of the program. In this approach, the evaluator focuses on the product and concludes what the original goals and objectives were. If the program is doing what it is intended to do, then the evaluator will likely confirm this. If the evaluator identifies new or different objectives, then there is a need to identify the causes of the unanticipated or unintended results.

There are numerous resources that provide information about objectives-oriented evaluations, including Alkin (1972); Christie and Alkin (2004); Fitzpatrick, Sanders and Worthen (2011); Gottman and Clasen (1972); Mathison (2005); Scriven (1974); Scriven (1980); Stufflebeam (1994); Stufflebeam and Coryn (2014); Stufflebeam and Shinkfield (1985) and Tyler (1942).

Needs Assessment

A needs assessment is defined by Mathison (2005) as

> ...a process or a systematic set of procedures undertaken for the purpose of setting priorities and making decisions about program or organizational improvement or allocation of resources. The priorities come from identified needs, which are measured discrepancies (gaps) between the current (what is) state of affairs of a group or organization and the desired (what should be) state in regard to variables of interest. (p. 276)

Needs assessments may identify and/or validate needs and establish priorities among them. The focus of needs assessments can be on objectives, individuals, groups, programs, products or initiatives (existing or planned). A needs assessment generally follows these steps:

- Identifying the need(s) to be studied
- Collecting opinions and data
- Analyzing the data and setting priorities among the needs
- Determining where/what action is needed
- Designing an action plan in response to the existing need

Methods used to conduct needs assessments often include surveys, focus groups, interviews, observation and analysis of existing documents or data.

Information about needs assessments can be obtained from several sources, including Gupta (1999); Mathison (2005); McCawley (2009); Stufflebeam and Coryn (2014); Stufflebeam, McCormick, Brinkerhoff and Nelson (1985); Watkins, West Meiers and Visser (2012) and Witkin and Altschuld (1995).

Appraisal and Accreditation

The appraisal and accreditation approaches emphasize judgement in relation to a set of criteria. The judgements are usually made by an expert or team of knowledgeable peers who examine a program or an aspect of a program, form opinions, draw conclusions and make recommendations. The expert or team may be from inside or outside the given organization, and the process may involve a component of self-evaluation. These approaches have been used in a variety of contexts. For example, many institutions/agencies (including large-scale assessment organizations, such as Ontario's Education Quality and Accountability Office) have used expert peer reviews (appraisals) to examine all or part of their programs, and for many years, the province of British Columbia used an accreditation model for its school accreditation program. Many professional organizations (e.g., AdvancED and the New England Association of Schools and Colleges, Inc. [US] and CfBT Education Trust [UK]) provide school accreditation services worldwide. Appraisals and accreditations may follow these general steps:

- Specifying the purpose of the appraisal or accreditation
- Identifying the expert or team of experts who will conduct the study
- Selecting or developing criteria (statements which describe what is "good" or "best of class" with regard to the program or component of the program being examined)
- Conducting an internal self-evaluation (Some evaluation designs include the program's staff doing a self-evaluation using the criteria and preparing a report of their findings.)
- Conducting the onsite evaluation (The expert or expert team conducts an on-site evaluation using the same criteria and forms initial impressions with reference to the internal report, if an internal self-evaluation was conducted.)

- Meeting to clarify impressions (If a self-evaluation was conducted, the appraisers meet with the self-evaluation team to clarify initial impressions and to communicate any necessary information.)
- Preparation of evaluation report (The appraisers prepare a final report with recommendations.)

This approach has a variety of uses but can be particularly helpful when self-evaluation is considered important, when immediate interpretation and feedback is desired and when interaction between the evaluators and program staff is considered important. Another model, criticism as evaluation, also relies on educational connoisseurs or expert evaluators.

Information about appraisals, accreditations and criticism as evaluation can be obtained from several sources, including the Council for National Academic Awards (1990); Eisner (1985a & b); Eisner (1994); Fretwell (2003); Maxwell (1996); Mathison (2005) and the National Study of School Evaluation (1979).

Judgement Evaluation of Intentions

The judgement evaluation of intentions approach examines what was intended with regard to a program's inputs (e.g., students, staff, qualifications, experience, materials, resources), operations (e.g., how the enterprise functions with regard to its activities, approaches, application of resources, interactions with clients) and outcomes (e.g., objectives, attitudes, achievements, impacts, costs), and then comparisons are made with the observed reality (What were the actual input factors? How did the program operate? What were the outcomes?). Considerations are given to whether there is a logical relationship among the program's intentions and whether or to what degree there is congruence between what was intended and what was observed.

Sometimes, comparisons are made between an existing program and some other standard. In this case, the evaluation questions focus on the extent to which the existing program meets or exceeds some standards, such as industry standards, those adopted by other well-recognized programs or those established by authoritative organizations (e.g., assessment or research associations).

More information about judgement evaluation of intentions (and also Robert Stake's responsive or stakeholder-centered evaluation approach) can be obtained from resources such as Mathison (2005); Stake (1967) and Stufflebeam and Coryn (2014).

Discrepancy Evaluation

In discrepancy evaluation, standards (stated objectives and expected outcomes) are established for each aspect of a program that is the focus of the evaluation. The actual performance (outcomes) of any given aspect/stage of a program is compared with the standard for that aspect. The evaluator looks for discrepancies or areas where improvement is required or desired. The steps of this type of evaluation are as follows:

- Determining the aspect(s) or stage(s) of a program to evaluate
- Establishing the standards (Some aspects/stages may have numerous standards, because there are several performances to be evaluated.)
- Comparing how the performance of the aspect/stage matches the given standard (Look for evidence of congruence and discrepancy.)
- Determining the reasons for any discrepancies
- Considering possible corrective actions or other decisions

This approach is particularly useful in evaluating pilot projects or new programs or diagnosing why things are not going well.

More information about discrepancy evaluation can be obtained from resources such as Mathison (2005) and Provus (1971).

Transactional Evaluation

The transactional evaluation approach (see also democratic evaluation, illuminative evaluation and responsive evaluation) is useful in determining the beliefs and feelings of those affected by an innovation or change, particularly if the change comes from outside the organization. If the effects of the change on the organization and people in it are not considered, the change may be unsuccessful. Transactional evaluation is designed to minimize the disruption and/or distress that can be caused by the threat of change or some dysfunction in an organization.

The following steps may be used in transactional evaluation:

- If the evaluation involves a new idea/change, the evaluator provides a detailed description of the proposed change to those who will be affected by it. Each person is asked to provide an anonymous response in which he/she indicates any positive and negative aspects of the change and any questions he/she would like answered. If the evaluation involves some perceived dysfunction, the evaluator asks each person affected to submit an anonymous report on what, in his/her opinion, is right and what is wrong with the current system.
- The responses received form the basis of a questionnaire of scaled responses to the views expressed.
- The questionnaire is distributed and returned.
- The results are tabulated and returned to the participants.
- The participants are brought together to discuss the change. (Skilled facilitators are recommended.) Those who are for the change act as proponents, and those against it act as critics.

(This allows the real strengths and weaknesses of the proposed change to surface before a trial implementation is conducted.)

- The trial/pilot implementation is conducted.
- All of the participants take part in re-evaluating the trial.
- Decisions are made in light of the re-evaluation.

More information about transactional evaluation can be obtained from resources such as Mathison (2005); Rippey (1975) and Stufflebeam and Coryn (2014).

Evaluation for Decision Making

Often the purpose of an evaluation is to provide information in support of decision making. Evaluation types can be categorized as: Context, Input, Process and Product (CIPP), and in combination, these evaluation types have been referred to as the CIPP evaluation model. Program evaluation can focus on a single category, or it may deal with any/all of the categories. Following are outlines of what an evaluation of each category entails.

Context Evaluation (What needs to be done?)

This type of evaluation attempts to do one or more of the following:

- Define the context or rationale of the program
- Indicate the target population
- Diagnose problems
- Determine objectives
- Identify objectives to be achieved
- Determine planning needs
- Provide a basis for judging outcomes

Input Evaluation (What can be done?)

This type of evaluation is concerned about the following aspects:

- Resources to achieve objectives
- Personnel involved
- Time allotments
- Organizational plans and procedures

Process Evaluation (What is being done?)

This type of evaluation describes how the activity is operating and provides information needed for the following types of decisions:

- Anticipating, identifying and overcoming procedural difficulties
- Making pre-program decisions
- Interpreting outcomes

Product Evaluation (What has been done?)

This type of evaluation collects descriptions and judgements of outcomes and relates them to objectives, context, input and process information to decide whether to continue, terminate, modify or adopt the activity or program.

Evaluation methods for the evaluation for decision making model might include comparative standards, test results, ratings, product reviews, group interviews, case studies and surveys.

More information about evaluation for decision making can be obtained from resources such as Mathison (2005); Stufflebeam (2000); Stufflebeam and Coryn (2014); Stufflebeam and Shinkfield (1985) and Stufflebeam and Webster (1988).

Adversarial Evaluation

This evaluation approach (see also judicial model of evaluation) is reminiscent of a legal trial, thus the name "adversarial." The model uses arguments for and against the program or the aspect(s) of the program that are the subject of the evaluation. Three groups are identified: the two adversary groups and a panel or jury. The panel should be impartial and possess some degree of expertise with respect to the program or aspect(s) of the program to be evaluated. The adversaries present their cases to the panel, which makes an evaluation and recommends subsequent action.

The following steps are part of an adversarial evaluation:

- **Preparation:** The adversaries prepare their cases for or against the proposal.
- **Confrontation:** The adversary teams present their cases until all contentions are presented. The contentions are usually based on need, practicality and desirability of the program or the aspect(s) of the program being evaluated. As each contention is presented, the opposing adversary team has the opportunity to cross-examine the other adversary team.
- **Resolution:** The panel questions the adversaries to gather additional information as required.
- **Recommendation:** The panel discusses the evidence in order to make judgements and recommendations, which are usually presented in a verbal and/or written report.

Adversarial (judicial) evaluation was among many approaches that proliferated during the 1970s. This approach, however, seems to have gone out of favour, for as Mathison (2005) states:

> **❝** Since the early 1980s … there seems to be no instances of a real-world application of the approach. The last full-on sighting may have been around 1980 and 1981 in the National Institute of Education's national hearing on minimum competency testing. (p. 214) **❞**

More information about adversarial evaluation can be obtained from resources such as Mathison (2005); Owens (1973); Popham and Carlson (1983); Stenzel (1976) and Wolf (1975).

Case Study Approach

Not every program or aspect(s) of a program can be evaluated by measuring the attainment of goals and objectives, noting discrepancies or by using instruments such as questionnaires. Sometimes evaluation purposes require a holistic portrayal of the program. In these instances, it is necessary to observe a program in action, often repeatedly, to get an accurate indication of how the program is working. In such instances, a case study approach may well be an appropriate one to use.

A case study usually relies on qualitative data-collection techniques. An observer (or observers) takes note of aspects of the program (e.g., how the program/aspect functions, working inter-relationships, how/why things happen the way they do) in its natural setting. Many aspects of a program may be explored using this evaluation approach, but the findings may not be generalizable to other settings. While it has many strengths, it must be recognized that the case study approach is often difficult to conduct and can be costly in terms of time and other resources.

There are several steps in conducting a case study as follows:

Pre-Fieldwork Stage (planning)

- **Establish the boundaries** (e.g., determine the program aspect(s) to be evaluated, set time frame for the evaluation)

- **Determine the unit of analysis** (e.g., in a school setting, will it be a single class, a grade, a subject area, a teaching method?)

- **Select a site or discuss sampling methods** (e.g., if sampling will it be simple random, cluster sample, stratified sample? or will sampling be purposeful such as extreme cases, typical cases, politically important or sensitive cases, cases displaying maximum variation, cases that are easily accessible?)

- **Establish contacts with the people in charge** (e.g., to encourage cooperation with the evaluation, assure those involved that the evaluation will be conducted honestly and that confidentiality and anonymity will be respected, convey information about how the evaluation will be conducted, inform participants about how the resulting information will be used)

- **Develop data-collection procedures** (e.g., observation and interviews are important sources of information, but other means such as document analysis, work samples, video/audio recordings may be involved; gathering data from various sources helps in cross-checking or triangulating information to ensure validity of results)

- **Develop methods for organizing the data** (e.g., data may come in a variety of forms, so categories of data, storage systems, coding systems need to be established)

Fieldwork Stage
(additional planning, training and data collection)

- **Training of staff** (e.g., observation forms and checklists may require development; staff involved in data collection may require training in observation, interviewing, video/audio recording and how to record their findings)

- **Fieldwork logistics** (e.g., who does what, scheduling of events, means of data recording, ordering of supplies)
- **Data collection** (e.g., some data collected through use of direct observation or interviews; other data collected by means of document analysis, records searching)

Data Analysis, Verification, Synthesis and Reporting Stage

- **Data analysis** (e.g., examining data for emerging issues or themes)
- **Verifying information** (e.g., cross-checking data from different sources for consistency of information/triangulation purposes to check the validity of results)
- **Synthesis of information** (e.g., interpreting the findings; sometimes useful to have a team/committee to review the information, discuss issues and results and reach common viewpoints/findings)
- **Develop the report** (e.g., the report provides a description of the study's evaluation issues and questions, methods, duration, limitations and findings)
- **Dissemination of evaluation findings** (results should be disseminated to those who need or want to know about the study's findings; planning committees are established to implement changes suggested by the evaluation results)

Information about the case study approach is available from numerous sources, including Lincoln and Guba (1985); MacDonald and Walker (1977); McNamara (2008b); Stake (1995) and Yin (2013).

Criticism as Evaluation (Connoisseurship)

Criticism is a form of qualitative evaluation that takes its lead from the work of critics in the arts. It is assumed the evaluator is a connoisseur: one who is competent enough to be able to make critical judgements. The critic creates a description of the situation that provides aspects that are in some way significant. What counts as significant depends on the theories, experience and values of the critic and his/her purposes. There are two aspects to criticism as evaluation:

The interpretive aspect (that asks what the situation means to those involved? How does this (element) operate? What ideas, concepts or theories can be used to explain its major features?)

The evaluative aspect (that answers the question: What is the importance or value of what is going on?)

Saskatchewan Education (1989) provides a brief example of a criticism as evaluation (connoisseurship) study in an education context.

A Saskatchewan school division, which sent its students across the provincial border to another school division, wanted to know the extent to which there was curriculum congruence between its Grade 10 curriculum and the Grade 10 curriculum in the other province. The evaluation was conducted as follows:

- Interviews were held with teachers, school and division administrators and students in both school divisions to gather data about the curricula and the impressions of students.

- Document reviews were conducted related to the curricula, school regulations and policy statements in both provinces.

- The evaluator, based on his expert opinion, drew conclusions and recommended a course of action with regard to the curriculum, the student group and the transfer of the students from one school to the other.

More information about criticism as evaluation is available in resources such as Eisner (1985a & b); Fitzpatrick, Sanders and Worthen (2011) and Stufflebeam and Coryn (2014).

The preceding descriptions of program evaluation approaches, adapted from Saskatchewan Education (1989), are oriented to evaluations of existing programs or their components. Evaluation in the form of a feasibility study (often including cost-benefit analysis) may also be conducted when a program/project is in the concept stage of development.

Feasibility Study

Hofstrand and Holz-Clause (2009) define a feasibility study as follows:

> ... a feasibility study is an analysis of the viability of an idea. The feasibility study focuses on helping answer the essential question of "should we proceed with the proposed project idea?" All activities of the study are directed toward helping to answer this question. (p.1)

Feasibility studies have many potential applications but are most commonly associated with business ventures. Clearly, it is advisable to determine whether or not a business concept is likely to succeed (be feasible) prior to investing time, effort and financial resources. According to Hofstrand and Holz-Clause (2009),

> A feasible business venture is one where the business will generate adequate cash-flow and profits, withstand the risks it will encounter, remain viable in the long-term and meet the goals of the founders. The venture can be either a start-up business, the purchase of an existing business, an expansion of current business operations or a new enterprise or an existing business. (p. 1)

A feasibility study is one important step in the process of developing a business concept. Pre-feasibility studies and market research may be conducted first to generate optional scenarios and sort out those that have potential from those that do not.

The University of Wisconsin Center for Cooperatives (1998) states that feasibility studies look at the following main areas:

1 | Market Issues

2 | Organizational Issues

3 | Technical issues

4 | Financial issues

The Center provides key questions (adapted here) for each of these three areas, which must be adequately answered before a project is feasible.

1 | Market Issues

✔ What is the current or projected demand for the proposed products/services?

✔ What are the target markets for the product/service?

✔ What is the projected supply in the area of the products/services needed for the project?

✔ What competition exists in this market?

✔ Is the location of the proposed project/business likely to affect its success?

2 | Organizational Issues

✔ What organizational structure is right for the project/business?

✔ What qualifications are needed to manage the project/business?

✔ Who will manage the project/business?

✔ What other staffing needs does the project/business have?

✔ Do you expect staffing needs to change over time? How?

3 | Technical Issues

- ✔ What are the technical needs for the proposed project/business?
- ✔ What equipment does the proposed project/business need?
- ✔ Where will this technology and equipment be obtained?
- ✔ When can the necessary technology and equipment be acquired?
- ✔ How much will the technology and equipment cost?

4 | Financial Issues

- ✔ What are the expected start-up costs (e.g., capital goods such as land, buildings and equipment)?
- ✔ What are the expected operating costs (e.g., ongoing costs such as rent, utilities and wages)?
- ✔ What are the revenue projections?
- ✔ What are the sources of financing (if required) for the project/business?
- ✔ What is the profitability projection for the proposed project/business?

A thorough feasibility study will provide a clear idea of whether or not the proposed project/business is a sound business concept. By itself, a feasibility study does not make business decisions. Instead, the purpose of a feasibility study is to generate sufficient information to support the decision-making process. The project/business leaders use this information to make the decision to implement, abandon or modify the business concept.

More information about feasibility studies can be obtained from resources such as Stevens (1982) and Stevens, Loudon, Sherwood and Dunn (2006).

CATEGORIZING AND EVALUATING PROGRAM EVALUATION APPROACHES

Various authors have developed classification schemas for program evaluation approaches. For example, Owen (2007) proposes a meta-model of five program evaluation forms: proactive, clarificative, interactive, monitoring and impact evaluation, each consisting of some of the more common evaluation approaches. Fitzpatrick, Sanders and Worthen (2011) classify the numerous program evaluation approaches into four categories based on their orientations: judgements of program quality, characteristics of the program, decisions to be made about the program and participation of stakeholders. Authors such as Worthen et al. (1997) provide an analysis of the characteristics, benefits, limitations and uses made of evaluation approaches; others rate approaches for modern-day evaluations (see Stufflebeam & Coryn, 2014, for example).

SUMMARY

Clearly, program evaluation may be conducted in a host of different ways depending on specific circumstances and needs. Each of the approaches brings something useful to the evaluation table that the evaluator can consider when determining the design of a program evaluation project. Regardless of the approach/model used, however, there are generic components to most evaluation studies, which are described in the following chapter.

PROGRAM EVALUATION PROCESS

4

INTRODUCTION

Regardless of the model or approach that is used, the process of program evaluation can be described by six general steps, illustrated by Figure 1 (page 46). The standards of practice and professional ethics should be considered at each stage and throughout a program evaluation study.

The first three steps relate to the planning process:

1 **Describe the program (including its goals/objectives) and identify the object and purposes of the evaluation.**

Once the evaluation team (consisting of participants with the required expertise) has been identified, it is important to first describe the program and the object of the evaluation in order to establish a clear framework for a program evaluation study prior to initiating any planning. The descriptions should include the purpose/rationale for the program including its goals and objectives, the intended recipients of the program, as well as other program elements such as its staff, resources, processes/activities and budget/costs.

Figure 1 | Program Evaluation Process

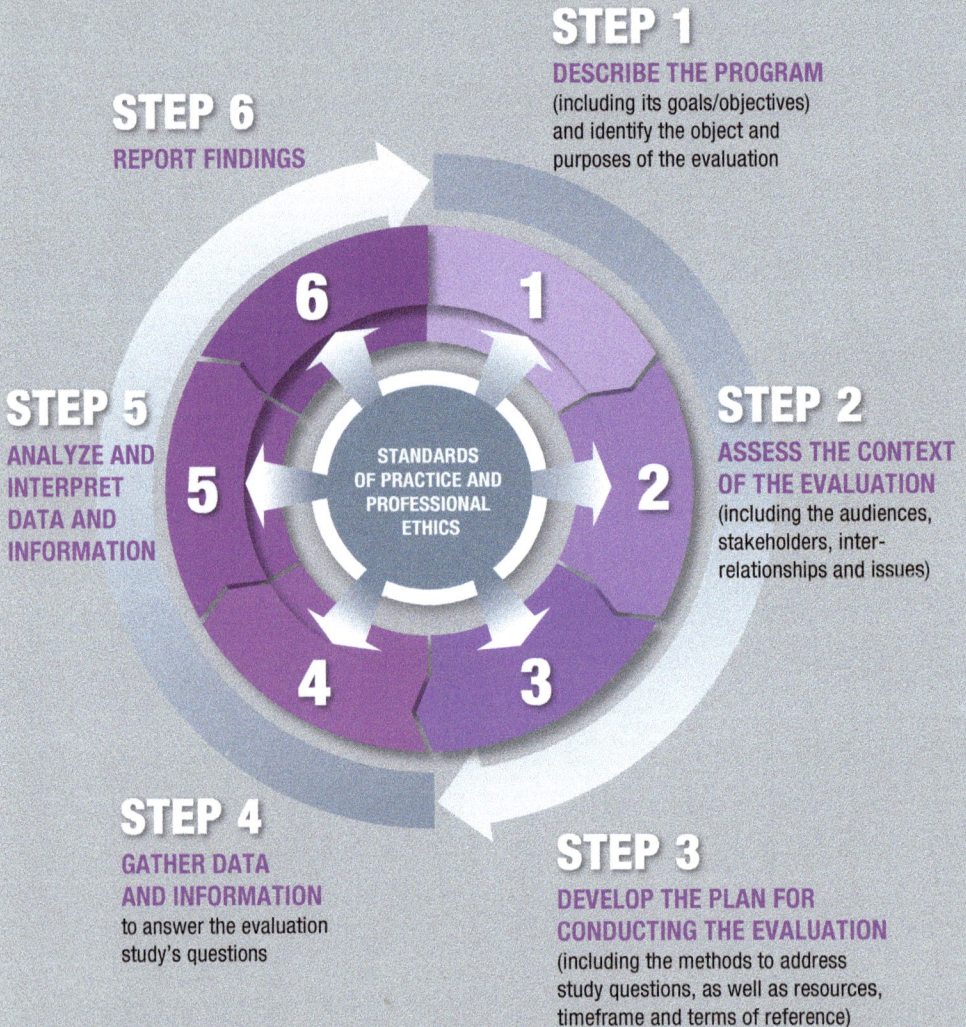

STEP 6
REPORT FINDINGS

STEP 1
DESCRIBE THE PROGRAM
(including its goals/objectives)
and identify the object and
purposes of the evaluation

STEP 5
ANALYZE AND
INTERPRET
DATA AND
INFORMATION

STEP 2
ASSESS THE CONTEXT
OF THE EVALUATION
(including the audiences,
stakeholders, inter-
relationships and issues)

**STANDARDS
OF PRACTICE AND
PROFESSIONAL
ETHICS**

STEP 4
GATHER DATA
AND INFORMATION
to answer the evaluation
study's questions

STEP 3
DEVELOP THE PLAN FOR
CONDUCTING THE EVALUATION
(including the methods to address
study questions, as well as resources,
timeframe and terms of reference)

It is also important to determine whether or not a plan for evaluation was articulated, and if so, what measures of program success were identified in the plan. (It is unfortunate that all too often, evaluation is not built into a program plan and is an afterthought.)

The purpose(s) of the evaluation, including the object(s)/aspects(s) of focus and the rationale for the perceived need for evaluation, must be established and documented. These are fundamental to developing the study's evaluation questions, which in turn inform how data/information can/should be gathered, analyzed and interpreted.

Working with the client and stakeholders and establishing good communications with all those who have a stake in the evaluation is crucial to the success of any program evaluation project. In the early stages, establishing strong relationships helps to ensure the program is well understood and goes a long way toward ensuring stakeholder buy-in. In addition, the relationship between the evaluator and client/sponsor must be well understood by all concerned, so that everyone's role is clear. For instance, will the evaluator be solely responsible for designing and conducting the study? Will the study be collaborative in nature in which the client/sponsor and/or stakeholders work as a team with the evaluator? Will the study be conducted by the client/sponsor and/or stakeholders with the evaluator serving as a guide?

2 Assess the context of the evaluation (including the audiences, stakeholders, inter-relationships and issues).

Steps one and two are not necessarily discreet; aspects of context will emerge as the program description and purpose(s) of the program evaluation are being documented. However, by identifying context as an evaluation stage, I am emphasizing its importance in evaluation for the purposes of this resource. Every evaluation project has a context (that is to say all of the circumstances surrounding it), and it is important that these elements be understood and documented if the program evaluation is to be successfully conducted. According to Holden and Zimmerman (2009),

> A successful evaluation is not only useful, practical, ethical and accurate, but it is also informed by an understanding of the special characteristics and conditions of each particular program. The evaluator needs to plan and conduct the study in the context of the program's people, politics, history, resources, constraints, values, needs and interests. (p. 10)

3 Develop the plan for conducting the evaluation (including the methods to address study questions, as well as resources, timeframe and terms of reference).

The involvement of stakeholders features prominently in much of the evaluation literature. Identifying who the stakeholders are and what their role(s) will be (if applicable) for a given program evaluation is critically important. Stakeholders may include individuals and/or groups such as the client/program sponsor, program staff, academics/experts in the given field and community members. As mentioned previously, the involvement of stakeholders early in the evaluation planning process is key to ensuring buy-in, and in addition, it is more likely that their needs will be met, and there will be no surprises when the evaluation report is released. Holden and Zimmerman (2009) state that

> the evaluator needs to define the role of the stakeholders in terms of the degree to which their input will be incorporated into the evaluation plan and their ongoing involvement in the evaluation once it is implemented. (p. 18)

The evaluation framework/plan is anchored in the specific evaluation questions to be answered. The evaluation questions, therefore, provide focus to the study. According to Saskatchewan Education (1989),

> **The evaluation framework...consists of a tree structure in which issues branch into questions and questions into indicators.** (p. 27)

The evaluation issues are the objects/aspects of focus (e.g., student academic achievement, student behaviour), but it is often challenging to identify and agree upon the specific issues to be addressed with the client/sponsor. Sometimes the client/sponsor has identified a program that requires evaluation and expects all questions about the program to be answered. This may be within the scope of the study; however, given practicalities such as budget, human resources and time, this may not be possible. In these cases, time is required upfront to work with the client/sponsor to determine what is feasible and to target specific aspects of the program for evaluation (what will and will not be evaluated).

Once the issues/objects/aspects of the evaluation have been established, the next step is to develop the research/evaluation questions. For example, the evaluation questions related to a study on an initiative to improve student academic achievement might be the following:

- How has students' academic achievement changed over time?
- Have all students benefitted from the initiative?

An evaluation question related to behaviour might be as follows:

- How has students' behaviour changed toward school/subject?

The indicators/measures related to achievement evaluation questions might be reflected by test scores over time and responses from teachers and parents to survey questions. The indicators related to behaviour might be reflected by responses from teachers and parents to survey questions, for example.

Once the general evaluation questions have been identified, the evaluator must develop the detailed work plan, which includes the:

- program evaluation approach to be used;
- comprehensive list of specific evaluation questions;
- data/information required to answer each question;
- source of that data/information;
- data/information collection methods;
- data/information collection arrangements (who? how? where? when?);
- data/information analysis and interpretation method(s) and
- reporting plan.

This is the stage in which elements of science and art come into play. Each evaluation question will require the collection of data/information for one or more variables. Given the budget, resources and time-frame of the study, the evaluator must select the most appropriate data-collection method(s). Evaluators need to determine whether or not readily available data/information already exists in sources such as public documents and databases, or whether other information sources will be required. Should it be necessary to collect original data, Fitzpatrick, Sanders and Worthen (2011) identify the following common sources:

- Program recipients (e.g., students, patients, clients, trainees)
- Program deliverers (e.g., social workers, therapists, trainers, teachers, physicians, nurse practitioners)
- Persons who have knowledge of the program recipients (e.g., parents, spouses, co-workers, supervisors)
- Program administrators

- Persons or groups who might be affected by the program or who could affect its operation (e.g., the general public, future participants, organizations or members of interest groups involved in the program)

- Policymakers (e.g., boards, CEOs, elected officials and their staffs)

- Persons who planned or funded the program (e.g., state department officials, legislators, federal funding agency officials)

- Persons with special expertise in the program's content or methodology (e.g., other program specialists, college or university researchers)

- Program events or activities that can be observed directly.

Once the evaluator has identified the source(s) of the required evaluation data/information, the next step is to determine the method(s) and instrument(s) to collect it. General data-collection methods, provided by Fitzpatrick, et al. (2011), are summarized as follows:

- **Data collected directly from individuals** in the form of self-reports of attitudes, opinions, behaviour, and personal characteristics using questionnaires/surveys, interviews, focus groups, as well as personal records such as diaries and logs and personal products such as tests (e.g., closed- and open-response answers) performances (e.g., simulations, debates, role-playing) and samples of work (e.g., portfolios, work products)

- **Data collected by independent observers** using open-ended observations and/or observation forms with checklists and/or rating scales

- **Data collected using technological devices** including audio and video recordings and photographs

- **Data collected from existing organizational information or formal repositories or databases** in the form of records, reports and documents of all types collected by various organizations (e.g., data reports, audit information, minutes of meetings, electronic mail)

Information about data-collection methods can be obtained from several sources, including Axinn and Pearce (2006); Fitzpatrick, et al. (2011); Olsen (2012); Stufflebeam and Coryn (2014) and Weller and Romney (1988).

The next three steps relate to conducting the evaluation:

4 Gather data and information to answer the evaluation study's questions.

Once the data-gathering methods and sources have been identified for each of the evaluation questions, other important elements must be addressed, such as sampling (whether or not sampling will be required in data collection and if so the type), human resources (the personnel who will gather the various types of data/information) and scheduling (when the data/information will be gathered).

If the study population is relatively small (e.g., the teaching staff of a school), then it would be generally advisable to include everyone in the study, because a sample may not generate representative data about the population. However, if the study population is relatively large, then sampling may well be appropriate, and a decision will need to be made as to the appropriate sampling type and size to be employed. If, for example, the program evaluation is focused on the nationwide needs for social services, literally millions of households could be considered part of the population of interest. In this instance, it would not be feasible to gather information from every household, so a representative sample could be drawn. On the other hand, if a particular sub-group, such as high-performance or low-performance schools were the focus of a program evaluation, then a purposeful sample might be an appropriate way to identify schools.

Program evaluations may be conducted by expert evaluators alone, or they may involve collaboration with various stakeholders, contractors (expert or non-expert) or volunteers. In the event that non-experts are involved in the evaluation, it is the responsibility of the evaluator to ensure that the individuals collecting data receive the appropriate training prior to data collection and that a system of checks are in place to ensure procedures are being followed faithfully during data collection. All participants in the evaluation should be familiar with *The Program Evaluation Standards* and *Guiding Principles for Evaluators,* and the *Standards* and *Principles* should be explicitly demonstrated in the program evaluation plan.

Timeliness in all its forms is essential in program evaluation. Usually, the evaluation study has a deadline(s) attached to it, that is to say a date(s) by which progress and final reports are to be delivered. These dates form the framework for the work-back schedule for data collection, analysis, interpretation and reporting. Fitzpatrick, et al. (2011) state that

> It seems almost a truism to say that evaluation information collected too late to bear on the relevant course of events is not useful. Timeliness is essential. In determining when information should be collected, evaluators should consider three criteria:
> - When will the information be needed?
> - When will the information be available?
> - When can the information conveniently be collected?
>
> Knowing when information will be needed establishes the latest allowable date for collecting it, because time must be allowed to analyze, interpret and report results. (p. 353)

5 Analyze and interpret data and information.

> **Analysis is the process of finding out what the collected information actually means. Analysis involves working with the data that have been collected to determine what conclusion these data support and how much support they provide for, or against, any conclusion. The purpose of analysis is to summarize from the information the message(s) it contains in order to make tentative conclusions or decisions."** (Saskatchewan Education, 1989, p. 39)

As part of the planning process, the evaluator needs to describe how the data/information will be analyzed for each evaluation question. Data analysis may involve quantitative (statistical) or qualitative techniques.

Once the data/information has been analyzed and statistical tables and/or summaries of the data have been generated, it is time to interpret the results. The consultations between the client/sponsor and evaluator and the agreements/understandings reached at the outset of the study will determine who will be involved in data interpretation. Data can speak in a variety of ways to different audiences; therefore, different people may have different interpretations of data. If the study design allows, it is therefore useful for the client/sponsor and/or key stakeholders to have an opportunity to review the information and participate in dialogue with the evaluator, so that different perspectives may be reflected in the final report.

Information about qualitative and quantitative data analysis can be obtained from several sources, including Fitzpatrick, et al. (2011); Miles and Huberman (2013); Ott and Longnecker (2008); Peck, Olsen and Devore (2011) and Stufflebeam and Coryn (2014).

---

6 Report findings.

Once the information has been collected and analyzed, the evaluation findings need to be communicated, and communication is the key word to emphasize in reporting. According to Saskatchewan Education (1989), the evaluation's audiences must be informed of the results, but the type of report and its contents may vary depending on the audiences' needs. For example, depending on the audience, reporting might be accomplished by means of press conferences/releases, newspaper articles, formal reports, executive summaries, meetings and discussions, presentations, direct mailings, letters/memoranda and audio-visual presentations.

If a formal, written report is required, the content should include the following components (adapted from Saskatchewan Education, 1989):

- **Introduction** that briefly explains the program's purposes and the reason for the evaluation

- **Program description** that provides in greater detail the rationale for the program, the program's objectives, the context of the evaluation and how and for whom the program operates

- **Evaluation description** that details the evaluation questions, information sources, design of the study, data-collection methods, data-analysis methods, timeframe for the evaluation study and any other understandings agreed to by the evaluator and client/sponsor

- **Results/Findings** related to each evaluation question

- **Recommendations** for action should be provided separate from the results

- **Appendices** may include information such as samples of data collection instruments, statistical tables, notes, work samples and references

More information about report writing can be obtained from resources such as Daniel (2012); Fitzpatrick, et al. (2011); Netzley and Snow (2001); Riordan (2013) and Stufflebeam and Coryn (2014).

An example evaluation work plan template is presented in Table 1.

SUMMARY

Program evaluation generally involves a six-step process:

1 | Describing the program
2 | Assessing the context
3 | Developing the plan
4 | Gathering the data/information
5 | Analyzing and interpreting the data/information
6 | Reporting the findings

Taking the time to clearly understand the evaluation context, establishing a good working relationship and communications with the client and stakeholders, adhering to rigorous, systematic processes and conducting the evaluation in accordance with *The Program Evaluation Standards* and the *Guiding Principles for Evaluators* will all contribute to successful program evaluation.

Table 1 | Sample Template: Evaluation Work Plan

Evaluation Questions/ Topics of Focus	Data/ Information Required	Source(s) of Data/ Information	Method of Collecting Data/ Information	Data/Information Collection Arrangements			Analysis of Data/ Information	Reporting		
				By Whom	Conditions	Timeline		Audience(s)	Method(s)	Timeline
QUESTION 1 / TOPIC 1										
QUESTION 2 / TOPIC 2										
QUESTION 3 / TOPIC 3										
QUESTION 4 / TOPIC 4										
QUESTION 5 / TOPIC 5										

Source: Adapted from Saskatchewan Education (1989) p.23; used with permission.

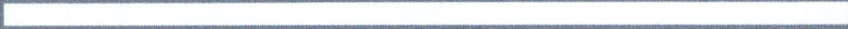

EXAMPLE CASES

Over the years, I have participated in many program evaluations. Among the evaluation models/approaches presented in Chapter 3, I have had personal experience with the following types of studies:

- Needs Assessment
- Feasibility Study
- Case Study
- Discrepancy Evaluation
- Evaluation for Decision Making
- Criticism as Evaluation (Connoisseurship)
- Objectives-Oriented Evaluation
- Appraisal
- Accreditation

Chapters 5 to 14 present example cases of program evaluation projects in which I have participated using the aforementioned program evaluation approaches. These cases demonstrate the methodologies used and how program evaluation standards of practice and ethical considerations were considered and incorporated into these evaluation studies.[3] Two case study examples are provided to describe the methodologies used in a small-scale evaluation study and a large-scale, multinational project.

---

[3] Information used to develop the example cases was obtained from a variety of sources, including the respective program evaluation final reports. Some of these reports, however, are not referenced in this book, because the clients required the studies' findings and recommendations be kept confidential, and the reports are not publicly available.

KINGDOM OF
SAUDI ARABIA

NEEDS ASSESSMENT

NEEDS ASSESSMENT
Study to Establish Social Institutions in Saudi Arabia

BACKGROUND AND CONTEXT OF THE STUDY

Situated in the Middle East, the Kingdom of Saudi Arabia occupies approximately 80 percent of the Arabian Peninsula. The Red Sea is located to the west of the country, and to the east is the Persian Gulf. The Kingdom shares borders with Jordan, Iraq, Kuwait, Qatar, the United Arab Emirates, the Sultanate of Oman and the Republic of Yemen.

In 1974, just four years before this study began, the first complete Saudi Arabian census was conducted (although the accuracy of the data has been questioned) in which information related to population numbers, family size and composition, gender and age distributions and social welfare issues was gathered. According to the United Nations Economic and Social Commission for Western Asia (2010), in 1980, the country's total Saudi national population (mostly ethnically Arab) was just under 10 million people, among whom two-thirds were urban dwellers and one-third were rural, and the working-age population was just over five million. In addition to the Saudi population, sizable numbers of Westerners, Arabs from other nearby countries and Asian expatriates were employed in the Kingdom. Until the 1960s, a large proportion of the population was seminomadic or nomadic. In the late 1970s, at the time of this study (and it continues to be the case today) the majority of the population inhabited the coastal strips and the three largest cities: Riyadh, Jeddah and Dammam. Administratively, the country was divided into 13 provinces and four regions: Asir (Southern Region), Al Hasa (Eastern Region), Hejaz (Western Region) and Najd (Central Region). The Northern Province was created around 1980 (refer to Figure 2).

Saudi Arabia was a highly conservative country that adhered to the Islamic religion and Sharia law. According to Metz (1993), the population was characterized by a high degree of cultural homogeneity, reflected by a common Arabic language and adherence to Sunni Wahhabi Islam, which had been fostered within the political culture promoted by the Saudi monarchy. Above all, the cultural homogeneity of the Kingdom rested in the diffusion of values and attitudes exemplified in the family and in Arabian tribal society, in particular the values and attitudes regarding relations within the family and the relations of the family with the rest of society. The family was the

Figure 2 | Kingdom of Saudi Arabia: Provinces and Surrounding Countries

Largest cities:

1. Riyadh
2. Jeddah
3. Dammam

most important social institution in Saudi Arabia. The structure of the family in Saudi Arabia was generally compatible with the structure of tribal lineage. Families were patrilineal; the boundaries of family membership were drawn around lines of descent through males.

According to Islamic law, men were permitted to marry as many as four wives. Among the adult generation of educated Western-oriented elites, polygyny was not commonly practiced; however, among some groups such as religious conservatives and the older generation (including the older generation within the royal family), it was more widespread. In the cities, polygynous households were more common among recent migrants from rural areas. For a family of means, a polygynous housing arrangement usually involved the husband providing a separate dwelling unit for each of his wives and her children.

These values and practices, as well as adherence to Islam, were fundamental to the cultural homogeneity among the Kingdom's diverse peoples, both tribal and non-tribal. Behaviour displaying generosity, hospitality, deference to those above in the hierarchy of the family, freedom from dependence on others, mastery over one's emotions and a willingness to support other family members were highly valued by the society. Chastity and sexual modesty were also very highly valued and expected. Applied primarily to women, these values were not only tied to family honour but were considered religious obligations as well. The veiling and separation of women from men were customary mechanisms to ensure sexual modesty. It also ensured the continuing dependence of women on men. Because the separation of women from unrelated men was accepted as a moral imperative, most activities of a woman outside her home required she be accompanied by a servant or a male relative.

The Kingdom being such a generous society, a broad array of individuals and organizations (including government agencies, community associations and charitable/benevolent societies) provided social welfare services to those with physical, intellectual and mental disabilities; people with health problems (including lepers); orphans; widows without income; juvenile delinquents; the elderly and those living in poverty (including beggars).

In 1970, Saudi Arabia began a series of Five-Year Plans meant to address various social, economic, infrastructure, manufacturing, defense and agriculture objectives. This evaluation study was conducted, for the most part, during the period of the Second Development Plan (1975-80) which contained numerous social goals (Metz, 1993).

PURPOSE OF THE STUDY

The fact that a great many organizations were delivering social welfare services was a very positive aspect of the society; however, there was no overall plan for how services could be effectively and efficiently delivered. In any given area, the same or similar services were being offered by multiple organizations. Consequently, the objective of this evaluation project, which was conducted during the period 1978 to 1981, was to determine the extent of need for a variety of social institutions across the Kingdom of Saudi Arabia, to develop a long-term plan for the effective and efficient delivery of social services and to make recommendations for its implementation.

RESEARCH QUESTIONS

The following research questions drove the study methodology:

- ✔ What social welfare services are being delivered in the various parts of the country?
- ✔ What organizations are delivering these services?
- ✔ Where are the services provided?
- ✔ Who should be delivering these services, and where should they be delivered?
- ✔ What is the level of satisfaction with the quality of the services provided?

- ✔ What efficiencies can be realized in the delivery of these services?
- ✔ What other social welfare services are needed?
- ✔ Who should deliver these services, and where should they be delivered?
- ✔ Are there geographic parts of the country where social welfare services are lacking?

THE STUDY TEAM

Following a Request for Proposals (RFP) competitive process, the Saudi Arabian Ministry of Labor and Social Affairs commissioned Planning Research Corporation's (PRC) Systems Sciences Company, a U.S.-based consulting firm, to conduct the program evaluation. The company assembled an experienced core team of seven male American and Canadian researchers with backgrounds in sociology, human geography, research, statistics and project management.

Among the Riyadh-based team were two individuals of the Islamic faith, one of whom had lived in the Middle East and had some facility in the Arabic Language. These team members were important to the success of the project, because in addition to their academic expertise and field experience, they provided information and advice to ensure cultural awareness and sensitivity. In addition to the full-time core team, PRC also secured the part-time services of five bilingual Arabic- and English-speaking consultants, four men and one woman (all academics and/or administrators), who lived in Saudi Araba at the time but whose home countries were Egypt, Jordan, Lebanon and Syria. These people were instrumental in assisting with the coordination of study activities.

EVALUATION METHODOLOGY

The program evaluation involved three data-collection methods:

1 **Literature reviews** to gain an understanding of the historical, social/cultural and political context, as well as the social institutions that would be the focus of the study

2 **Interviews with senior officials** of the Ministry of Labor and Social Affairs and the directors (heads) of social institutions nationwide to obtain their perspectives on the issues and suggestions to improve the delivery of social services

3 **A national household survey** to gather information about the social services used and/or required, satisfaction with the existing services and indications about where and how improvements could be made

Literature Reviews

Prior to its arrival in Saudi Arabia, and for the first three or four months in-country, the study team reviewed research reports and other literature pertaining to the Kingdom's organizational/administrative structure, culture, society and social institutions. These reviews were summarized to provide a detailed context for the evaluation project. Although a high-level research methodology had been developed well in advance of the team's arrival in Saudi Arabia, the information gleaned from the literature reviews was helpful to the team in refining many aspects of the study.

Interviews with Senior Officials

During the time that literature reviews were being conducted, the team held meetings concurrently with senior officials of the Ministry of Labor and Social Affairs. These meetings were critically important to the success of the study because they provided opportunities to

- meet the key personalities and establish a good working relationship with the client;
- clarify details of the study's purposes and scope;
- obtain additional political and cultural contextual information relevant to the study;
- discuss and negotiate aspects of the methodology including any limitations;
- gain understandings and/or clarifications of the administrative structure of the Kingdom and social service providers, as well as the proper protocols to follow when contacting and interacting with them;
- acquire letters of introduction for use with the relevant organizations and stakeholders to ensure their cooperation with the study team and
- determine the types and schedule of reports required by the Ministry.

In addition to providing letters of introduction, The Ministry of Labor and Social Affairs contacted the governors of the 13 provinces to introduce the study and research team and to ask for their cooperation in the study. Following the preliminary meetings with the Ministry, the evaluation team finalized the study's methodology. Every four months, the team held briefings with senior Ministry officials and submitted progress reports. (Six copies in Arabic and six in English were required.) This process ensured transparency and provided a mechanism to ensure the client's needs were being met, to avoid any surprises and to give the Ministry confidence that the project was proceeding on schedule.

Once the details of the study methodology were finalized, the project team commenced semi-structured interviews with the directors (heads) of an array of government agencies, community associations and non-profit charitable organizations that provided social welfare services across the country. The objective was to obtain their perspectives on who their clients were, who else was delivering the same or similar services, the relative success of their organizations in service delivery, the challenges they were encountering and any suggestions they had to improve the delivery of services to those in need. For reasons of efficiency, this work was conducted concurrently with the national household survey.

National Household Survey

Challenges

The national household survey was the most elaborate and expensive aspect of the study, and there were unique challenges associated with it as follows:

- Telephone, telegraph and telex services existed in the Kingdom at the time of the study, but not everyone had access, and there were no reliable directories identifying households with access to telecommunications services.

- Although there were good estimates of population for most urban areas, specific householders' names and addresses were unavailable.

- In many rural areas, street maps and population distributions within the towns/villages were unavailable.

- There were only estimates of the locations and numbers of the predominantly desert-dwelling, nomadic Bedouin people.

- The holy cities of Mecca and Medina were off-limits to non-Muslims (which meant most of the study team).

- Only one member of the core team had any facility with the Arabic language.

- All members of the study team were male and were therefore unable to be in the physical presence of Saudi women, let alone interview them.

- In the years prior to this study, there had been two attempts to conduct a national census. It had proven challenging to gain the cooperation of citizens in these studies, as interview surveys were uncommon, and the people were skeptical about/suspicious of their intent.

The Survey

Access to households by telephone may have been the most efficient means of conducting interviews had there been universal access and if reliable household directories had been available. In any case, the study team believed that face-to-face contact would result in better response rates and higher-quality information. (It is more difficult for a prospective respondent to refuse participation if the interviewer presents him/herself in person.) Furthermore, by interviewing people in person, the interviewers were able to explain the value of the study both to society and the individual, as well as answer any questions. Taking the time to put the interviewees more at ease and reassuring them that their involvement in the survey was worthwhile, proved effective in securing high response rates.

In general, the national household survey included

- checklists to record the numbers, ages, occupations and education levels of household members;

- checklists to indicate the social service(s) (if any) the inter-viewees or members of their households were receiving;

- open-response questions to gather information about who de-livered the service(s) and where the service was delivered (e.g., institution, home, community development centre);

- open-response questions to ask who should be delivering the service(s) and why;

- Likert scales to express respondents' level of satisfaction with the service(s) provided;

- an open-response question asking what social services/other services were needed and

- open-response questions asking who should deliver the needed service(s), where they should be delivered and why (if applicable).

The interviews (conducted in Arabic) were structured in that the in-terviewer asked the same questions to all respondents; however, in-terviewers were permitted to probe for more in-depth information, particularly with the open-response questions. The information ob-tained from interviewees was kept confidential; no names were as-sociated with the surveys. The location of the households, with ref-erence to the community and a grid system, was recorded for later analysis. Prior to launching the "live" national household survey, the questions were pilot-tested with a convenience sample of about 30 respondents from the Riyadh area. Based on the pilot experience, adjustments were made to the survey instrument.

The Interview Teams

Each of four members of the core study team assumed responsibility for interviewing in a given region. Because only one member of the study team had any facility with the Arabic Language, translators were hired on a temporary basis to work directly with each study team member. Furthermore, one contracted, bilingual consultant was attached to the interview team in each region. These consultants provided necessary liaison services with local officials/administrators to ensure interviews could proceed uninterrupted, and they also assisted with recruiting and training interviewers. As was mentioned earlier, the holy cities of Mecca and Medina were inaccessible to most of the study team, and so leadership of the interview process became the responsibility of the consultants in these urban centres.

A total of approximately 200 male and female Saudi Arabian university students were employed as interviewers. Female interviewers were essential to the study, because according to custom only women were permitted to interview adult females. The female consultant was responsible for coordinating interviews with women. The students, about 50 of whom were sent out to interview in each region, had at least some field experience and received thorough training from the study team and consultants prior to "live" interviewing.

Sampling Procedures

The framework for the survey required a random sample of households across the country. In the absence of household address directories by community, the evaluation team had to be creative in establishing a sampling plan. At the time of the study, there were approximately 1.6 million Saudi national households in the Kingdom. The study team determined that a two percent national sample, or about 32,000 households, would provide valid and reliable data upon which to base conclusions and recommendations. As was mentioned in the Background and Context section, in 1978, the country was divided into four regions and 13 provinces. These administrative areas were used as sampling strata. Approximately 8,000 households were to be interviewed in each of the four regions, and within each region, the number of households to be interviewed in each province and community was proportional to its estimated population.

Once the study team had established the number of interviews to be held in each community, "random sampling" of households was conducted. It was necessary to use land-use maps (where they existed) of local communities, which provided the locations of commercial and residential buildings, because directories of householders' names and addresses were unavailable. A fine grid system was superimposed on such maps, and depending on the number of interviews to be conducted in the community, a given number of interviews was assigned to randomly selected grids. The interview teams were then dispatched to locate the chosen residential areas and conduct the interviews.

In many rural areas, maps of small towns and villages were non-existent. In such cases, the study team resorted to sketching maps of the communities' street, commercial and residential patterns in order to apply the grid system for sampling purposes. If there was no adult household member available at the first attempt, the interview team was expected to call back for a second time before opting to replace the household with another in the same area. Not only was the grid system useful in selecting residential areas to conduct interviews, but also the grid coordinates identified the geographic location of each interview within the country. These grid references were recorded on each interview survey for future analysis purposes.

Another segment of the Saudi population that the team attempted to include in the study was the Bedouin. Over the years, the government had been encouraging these desert dwellers to abandon their nomadic lifestyle in favour of a more modern one in the urban areas. These attempts had been somewhat successful; however, during the 1970s and 80s when this study was conducted, a sizeable number of Bedouin still occupied tracts of desert throughout the country, including the Rub' al Khali (Empty Quarter) in southeastern Saudi Arabia. Establishing a credible sampling frame for this group was not possible, because accurate population numbers were unavailable, and because these people were constantly on the move. The study team therefore decided that attempts would be made, though local officials/administrators, to interview the Bedouin when they appeared in the vicinity of urban centres. Learning that large groups of nomads had appeared in relatively accessible areas to the southwest of Dammam and near the northern city of Al-Jawf, the Eastern and Central Regions' interview teams, respectively, journeyed out to survey members of these tribes and to ascertain their migratory patterns.

DATA CODING, ANALYSIS AND INTERPRETATION

Because the interview sampling plan allowed for callbacks and household replacements, the response rate was very high: over 90 percent. As a result, more than 28,000 responses were available for analysis.

Clearly, the interviews generated a great deal of data/information that needed to be organized and reduced prior to analysis. Data reduction was accomplished by coding in two stages. Once the surveys had been initially developed, pre-coding (assigning number codes to answer categories prior to interviewing) was conducted for the checklists (essentially yes/no categories) and five-point Likert scales ("strongly agree" to "strongly disagree"). After data collection (post-coding), the study team developed a coding system in order to classify the data derived from the semi-structured interviews with directors (heads) of government agencies, community associations and non-profit charitable organizations that provided social welfare services, as well as the open-response questions from the national household survey. Developing the codes was a laborious process in which the Arabic-speaking core team member and consultants examined several hundred survey forms to generate response categories. This process of reviewing the completed surveys continued until no new response categories emerged. Each response category was given a code number for computer analysis, and then several Saudi university students were hired to apply the codebook to all survey responses.

Keypunching, data cleaning and analysis, interpretation and final report writing were conducted at PRC headquarters in McLean, Virginia. Various types of statistical analyses were conducted for the country as a whole, by region and by province. They included

- descriptive statistics such as mean, median, mode;
- measures of association/relationship between/among variables (e.g., correlational studies: bivariate, partial and multiple correlations, multiple regressions) and
- factor analyses.

REPORTING

According to the terms of the agreement with the Saudi Arabian Ministry of Labour and Social Affairs, PRC Systems Sciences Company was obligated to provide a final report to the Ministry; no other stakeholders were to be given information about the study's findings and recommendations. The final study report (12 copies in Arabic and six in English were required) provided a comprehensive picture of the current state of social service delivery at that time, including

- the social welfare services that were available;
- the organization(s) that were delivering the service(s);
- each organization's catchment/service area(s), indicating where there were overlapping services;
- the level of satisfaction with the service(s) offered and
- areas where service(s) were unavailable or insufficient.

The report included a long-range plan for social institutions in the Kingdom, including recommendations and rationales related to

- the existing institutions/organizations that should continue offering social services and in some cases be expanded;
- the existing institutions/organizations that should discontinue offering the service(s);
- where, specifically, the social service(s) should be located and
- new institutions and services and where they should be located.

The study team generated maps (to accompany the text) that demonstrated the recommended social services delivery system, including the catchment areas for each service. Providing both text and graphic displays in the report was a powerful way of demonstrating the efficiency and effectiveness of the recommended plan.

SUMMARY

The Study to Establish Social Institutions in Saudi Arabia incorporated many of the elements that comprise *The Program Evaluation Standards* and *Guiding Principles for Evaluators.*

- The project was managed effectively and included qualified individuals with appropriate technical expertise and field experience, as well as a good understanding of the local culture.

- By conducting thorough literature reviews and holding extensive consultations with Ministry officials and local project coordinators, the team was well-prepared to develop the final study design and conduct fieldwork.

- The confidentiality of participants' personal information was safeguarded.

- The study design proved to be successful in that it generated suitable information with which to answer the research questions and formulate appropriate conclusions and recommendations; the final report was well-received by the client.

- One important lesson learned, however, related to translation. As was mentioned earlier, briefings and progress reports were required every four months. The first Arabic progress report was translated from English in Washington, D.C. by an Egyptian translator. It came as a surprise to the study team when the client was unhappy, not about the content of the report but because the Arabic Language usage was inappropriate for Saudi Arabia. For the duration of the study, at least two professional Saudi Arabic translators were hired to translate and back translate all reports before they were submitted to the client.

**KINGDOM OF
SAUDI ARABIA**

FEASIBILITY STUDY

FEASIBILITY STUDY
Feasibility Study of the Jamjoom Commercial Center

6

BACKGROUND AND CONTEXT OF THE STUDY

The Kingdom of Saudi Arabia occupies approximately 80 percent of the Arabian Peninsula. Its neighbours to the north include Jordan, Iraq and Kuwait, with the Yemens and Oman bordering the nation to the south. The Persian Gulf and the Red Sea form the eastern and western boundaries, respectively (refer to Figure 2, page 65). Saudi Arabia's position as a world-leading exporter of petroleum has led to rapidly increasing prominence for the Kingdom in economic and political circles. Politically, its moderate and stable monarchial government is perhaps the most influential in the Middle East. Attainment of the Kingdom's international economic position has generated extensive investment interest within Saudi Arabia on the part of Saudis and foreign nationals. The dominant majority of Saudi Arabia's national income is traceable to the petroleum industry and is mainly responsible for the intensive infrastructure development in the Kingdom.

In addition to its economic and political stature, Saudi Arabia (and specifically the two holy cities of Mecca and Medina) is the spiritual focus of millions of Muslims worldwide. Each year, more than a million Hajjis (pilgrims) travel from all parts of the Islamic world to visit these holy places.

Saudi Arabia's economic expansion was to a large extent defined and governed by a series of national Five-Year Plans. These plans served as blueprints for the programmed national development. At the time of this study (1980), the Kingdom was nearing the end of the second of these Five-Year Plans, which covered the period 1975 to 1980. During this time, much of the Kingdom's infrastructure was developed through massive construction programs creating and greatly expanding port and airport facilities; numerous government, education and health care facilities; transportation systems and related installations. The momentum of the second Five-Year Plan was expected to carry over into the third Plan. Emphasis in the third Five-Year Plan was to be on maintenance of existing facilities and human resource development. Industrial and commercial enterprise investments, improved public sector management and general limits and controls upon future increases in foreign manpower levels were also expected to be stressed.

Saudi Arabia is made up of four economically prominent regions:

- The Hejaz (site of Jeddah, one of the Kingdom's primary commercial centres and gateway to Mecca and Medina)
- The Asir (the relatively fertile strip of coastal mountains in the extreme southwest bordering Yemen)
- The Najd (the vast, arid plateau in the centre of the Arabian Peninsula containing Riyadh, the Kindom's capital city)

- Al Hasa (the location of Saudi Arabia's major oil and natural gas reserves in the Eastern Region)

A census taken in 1974 found Riyadh to be the nation's leading population centre. Jeddah, Mecca, Ta'if (the unofficial summer capital) and Medina, all located within the Western Region, were also included among the country's five largest cities. Jeddah is located on the Red Sea coast of Saudi Arabia, about midway between the bordering nations of Jordan and Yemen. The city, situated on a 12-kilometre coastal plain, is bordered inland by the foothills of the Saudi Arabian Massif.

Jeddah is the leading commercial and population centre of the Western Region and the Kingdom's major air and sea point of entry for passenger and cargo arrivals. The national development program and resulting extensive demand for consumer goods, construction materials and technical and administrative services in the region gave dramatic impetus to Jeddah's physical and economic development. With the completion of what was at the time the world's largest airport, as well as extensive expansion of the Jeddah seaport, the city's role as a major international gateway to the Kingdom became increasingly prominent.

PURPOSE OF THE STUDY

At the time of the study, the Jamjoom family of Jeddah, Saudi Arabia held an interest in three adjoining parcels of land, totaling more than three hectares, in the Al Hamra-Ruwais section of the city. Located immediately east of the Jeddah Intercontinental Hotel (which was under construction), and in close proximity to the Jeddah Corniche beachfront area on the Red Sea, the parcels represented what was thought to be a prime commercial location in a developing prestige

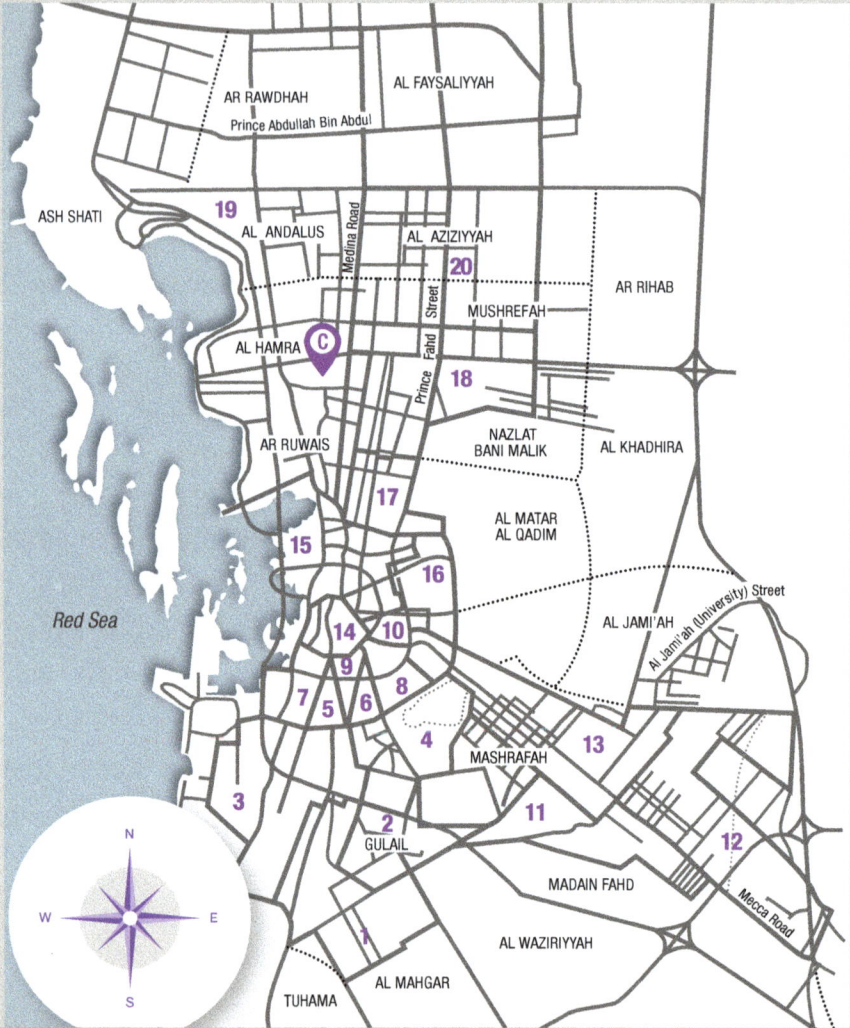

Figure 3 | Population Sectors (Haras) Jeddah and Location of Proposed Jamjoom Commercial Center

1	Karantina	8	Sabeel	15	Baghdadia & Amaria
2	Gulail	9	Harat Barra	16	Kandara
3	Gurayat & Thalba	10	Sahaifa	17	Sharafia
4	Nuzla Yamania	11	Nusla Sharkia	18	Bani Malik
5	Bukharia	12	Kilo 6–10	19	Ruwais, Hamra, Medina Road
6	Hindawia	13	Kilo 1–5	20	Mushrefah
7	Shati	14	Al Yaman & Asham	C	Location of proposed Jamjoom Commercial Center

area (refer to Figure 3). The family proposed to utilize these parcels for development of an extensive three-level commercial complex featuring a regional shopping centre of approximately 53,000 square metres and professional office suites totaling approximately 45,000 square metres. The shopping centre was conceived as an all-year, indoor commercial and social gathering place creating a pleasant, climate-controlled environment in which patrons could spend several hours shopping, dining and engaging in related activities. A cinema and child-care centre were among ancillary facilities included in the design. As part of the overall development planning process, the Jamjooms retained Economics Research Associates (ERA), a subsidiary of Planning Research Corporation, to conduct a feasibility study. ERA's study, in general terms, was to do the following:

- Define, from an economic perspective, the general market conditions of Jeddah and the Jamjoom site area
- Measure the current and anticipated market support for a regional-scale retail shopping centre and modern office complex within the project area, with attention given to retail and office absorption potentials and financial performance

RESEARCH QUESTIONS

The following research questions were the foundation of the Jeddah Jamjoom Commercial Center site feasibility study:

- ✔ What are the population trends and projections?
- ✔ What are the employment patterns, trends and projections?
- ✔ What are the personal income patterns, inflation rates and cost of living?
- ✔ What are the motor vehicle registration and traffic patterns and trends?

- ✔ What are the patterns and trends in commercial airline traffic?

- ✔ What are the trends with regard to port capacity and flow of imports?

- ✔ What are patterns and trends in retail expenditures, including business travelers and Hajjis?

- ✔ What are the land-use patterns and trends?

- ✔ What are the site characteristics?

- ✔ How accessible and visible is the proposed site?

- ✔ What is the proposed site's current and projected trade area potential?

- ✔ What are the general retail and office market current conditions and projections?

- ✔ What are the competitive and complementary impacts of current and future retail and office development in the local and regional area?

- ✔ How should the retail and office mall be designed and configured? What should the tenant mix be?

- ✔ What should the rental structure be?

- ✔ What is the expected shopper composition, and what are their preferences?

- ✔ What are the parking requirements for the Jamjoom project?

- ✔ What are the expected costs (development of the centre, lease commissions, operating expenses, financing/debt service)?

- ✔ What is the expected revenue (lease income)?

- ✔ What is the expected financial performance (cash flow: sources and uses of funds) for the first ten years of operations?

THE STUDY TEAM

The feasibility study was conducted over a ten-month period by a four-person team, which included ERA's Senior Vice President who served as project manager (both directing and participating in the research project), two seasoned ERA economists and an experienced field researcher. During the research process, ERA also sought and received information from numerous local, regional and external sources. Saudi translators were hired to accompany the study team as required and to translate documents.

EVALUATION METHODOLOGY

Prior to conducting research, the study team held extensive meetings with the President of the Jamjoom organization to discuss data/information requirements and potential sources of the data. Once the range of data sources had been identified, the Jamjooms made contact with the various Saudi Ministries to introduce the project and study team, secure the Ministries' cooperation and obtain the name of a key contact person at each Ministry who would provide relevant documents and data. The preliminary planning meetings and contacts with Ministry officials took place during the first two months of the project. The client expected progress reports and briefings at the end of the third and sixth months; the final report was to be submitted at the end of the tenth month.

Document and Data Reviews

Document and data reviews were the primary data-collection methods used in this study. As was mentioned previously, data and information was gathered from existing documents and databases obtained from various local, regional, national and external sources, including the Saudi Arabian Ministries of Interior, Finance and National Economy, Municipal and Rural Affairs, Planning, and the Central Department of Statistics. Data and information were also obtained from the Urban Land Institute and Planning Research Corporation's and Economics Research Associates' proprietary sources. Many private firms and individuals, possessing specific market knowledge and expertise, also made contributions to the study.

Field Research

Although documents and databases were the principal sources of data and information for the evaluation, the study team spent a significant amount of time conducting field visits and analysis. For instance, the team visited the proposed development site and surrounding area to appreciate the site characteristics (e.g., access, visibility, surrounding land uses), to observe traffic flows on the road systems at various times of the day and to inquire about current and projected business activity in the area during visits to local retail and commercial businesses.

DATA ANALYSIS AND INTERPRETATION

Documents and data from all available sources were gathered and analyzed to answer each of the study's research questions. The following types of data and information were collected for the city of Jeddah and the proposed Jamjoom Commercial Center:

- Personal income patterns
- Population estimates by district
- Population projections
- Population by nationality
- Employment and unemployment estimates and projections

- Cost of living index for urban households
- Motor vehicle registrations
- Airline passenger traffic
- Port capacity statistics
- Annual pilgrimage totals to Mecca and other holy places
- Major hotel development activity
- Competitive inventory (e.g., rentable area, number of parking spaces, annual lease rates, percent occupied of other commercial centres)
- Population projections, Jamjoom Commercial Center trade area
- Average annual wages by nationality for private business establishments
- Current and projected annual per capita income, Jamjoom Commercial Center trade area

REPORTING

Following data collection, the study team analyzed the information and generated primarily descriptive statistics related to the Jamjoom Commercial Center trade area in response to the research questions. These statistics were presented in tabular format in the final report. In addition to the aforementioned data, ERA generated the following types of information, related to the Jamjoom Commercial Center trade area, for inclusion in the final report:

- Projected expenditure potential as a percentage of per capita income
- Projected capture potential by type of outlet (estimated percentage and revenue)

- Growth expectations in selected office-using markets (e.g., education and training, medical/health care, building maintenance, industrial and commercial partnerships, business and investment, clerical and marketing, financial services, insurance industry)
- Projected regional office space demand
- Projected regional office space capture potential
- Sizing recommendations (square metres) by type of outlet
- Composition by tenant classification (type of outlet), including percentage of space, percentage of sales and expected income from tenants
- Parking space recommendations
- Projected financial performance (sources and uses of funds) over a ten-year period including income (lease income) and costs (development, lease commissions, operating expenses, tenant improvements and financing/debt service)
- Recommendation on the feasibility of the land development project

The final report was assembled and printed at the ERA head office in San Francisco, California. In accordance with the contractual arrangements, at the end of the ten-month period, ERA submitted six copies of the final report (in English and in Arabic) to the Jamjoom organization in conjunction with a summary briefing.

SUMMARY

The feasibility study of the proposed Jamjoom Commercial Center in Jeddah, Saudi Arabia reflected the standards of best practice in *The Program Evaluation Standards* and *Guiding Principles for Evaluators.*

- The Jamjoom Organization commissioned Economics Research Associates, a company experienced in providing economics analysis and planning consulting services to a wide variety of clients in both the public and private sectors. The study team comprised experts in project management, economics and research.

- The work of the small team was well-managed; each member had specific research assignments and deliverables.

- Establishing good communications and a strong working relationship with the client was fundamental to the study. Pre-data-collection meetings and regular progress reports were instrumental in ensuring the requirements of the feasibility study were clearly understood, relevant data and information sources were identified and effective connections with key Ministry and local officials were established.

- Through the process of providing regular progress reports and briefings, there were no surprises for the client when the final report was submitted. In all aspects, the client was pleased with the final report and the process by which it was developed.

BRITISH COLUMBIA

CASE STUDY A

CASE STUDY A
Organizational Culture of Three High Performance Secondary Schools in British Columbia

BACKGROUND AND CONTEXT OF THE STUDY

At the time this study was conducted (1989-1991), for more than half a century, researchers had attempted to answer the question as to whether or not schools made a difference to students' educational development. Some research, conducted during the 1960s and 1970s, for example, showed that factors external to the school, such as socioeconomic status and ethnic origin, were more likely to impact student outcomes than internal school factors (see Coleman, Campbell, Hobson, McPartland, Mood, Weinfeld & York, 1966 and Jencks, Smith, Acland, Bane, Cohen, Gintis, Heyns & Michelson, 1973, for example).

Other research, however, demonstrated that organizational climate (described by recurring patterns of behaviour, attitudes and feelings that were characteristic of life in the organization) and ethos/culture (described by elements such as teachers' behaviour at work, expectations for student performance, rewards for student success and the extent to which students were allowed to take responsibility) were associated with higher levels of student academic achievement, attendance and better behaviour (see Rutter, Maugham, Mortimore & Ouston, 1979, for example).

Summarizing the research, Jones (1991) stated that

> **For decades, researchers have conducted studies to identify factors which positively relate to student educational outcomes. The ability to measure educational performance and to relate it to its determinants has been regarded as important for designing policies relating to school effectiveness, teacher accountability and educational finance. The emergence of the effective schools movement in the 1970s, and the recent work being conducted on educational indicators ... demonstrate the continuing interest in finding appropriate measures of the outcomes of schooling and the factors that relate to them.** (p. 2)

Although school climate had been the subject of numerous research studies, mainly related to leadership and administration, at the time, fewer studies had been conducted on the culture of high performance schools. One study, conducted by Saphier and King (1985), suggested that school improvement was the combination of four key elements:

- Increasing teacher skills
- Conducting systematic review and renewal of curriculum
- Strengthening school-community partnerships by meaningfully involving parents and other members of the public
- Effecting organizational improvement

The authors contended that the concept of school culture was at the foundation of all four elements, and therefore, culture was fundamental to school improvement and student success.

In a summary of the literature on school culture, conducted by Van Sant O'Neill, Cohen, Hadikin, Koretchuk, Price and Swenson (1988), the authors stated that

> **"** ...schools can become more effective if they develop the right kind of culture and that dysfunctional cultures can be changed in order to adapt better to environmental realities. (p.1) **"**

Furthermore, some research suggested that strong school organizational cultures could be created (see Deal & Kennedy, 1982; Johnston, 1987; Ouchi; 1981 and Peters & Waterman, 1982, for example).

PURPOSE OF THE STUDY

At the time this study was conducted, there was some evidence to suggest that strong, positive school cultures were characteristic of high performance schools, and that an important leadership function was the creation and management of organizational culture.

The general purpose of this study, therefore, was to describe the organizational cultures of three high performance secondary schools in British Columbia (B.C.) and to identify similarities and differences among them. By investigating the cultures of high performance schools and by comparative analysis, this research was meant to provide a documentary resource for educational theorists and practitioners. It was also anticipated that answers to the research questions could have implications for leadership training in general and for preparation of secondary-school principals in particular. (It should be noted, however, that because this case study was conducted in three secondary schools, conclusions drawn could only apply directly to the three study schools and could not necessarily be generalized to other secondary schools.)

RESEARCH QUESTIONS

The study's guiding research questions were as follows:

- ✔ Do common cultural values exist among the high performance schools?

- ✔ Do common cultural attitudes exist among the high performance schools?

- ✔ Do common cultural norms exist among the high performance schools?

- ✔ Do student, teacher, administrator, parent and secretary/custodian perceptions of the school's organizational culture vary?

- ✔ Is there less divergence among student, teacher, administrator, parent and secretary/custodian perceptions of the school's organizational culture in the independent as compared to the public schools?

- ✔ Is the independent school characterized by a stronger organizational culture than the public schools?

- ✔ Is the rural public school characterized by a stronger organizational culture than the urban public school?

- ✔ Does the perception of organizational culture vary with the length of time the individual has been associated with the school?

THE STUDY TEAM

The study was conducted by an educator with many years of elementary- and secondary-school experience as a classroom teacher and administrator. In addition, the individual was knowledgeable in data-gathering and analysis techniques and was experienced in conducting field research, particularly surveys and interviews.

EVALUATION METHODOLOGY

Literature reviews, semi-structured interviews and document reviews were selected as the principal methods of data/information collection.

Literature Reviews

Over the course of approximately one year, the researcher conducted extensive literature reviews on topics related to organizational culture (e.g., climate, ethos, values, underlying assumptions, style) and research approaches to uncover and describe organizational culture, particularly in schools.

Based on the literature reviews, for the purposes of the study, organizational culture was defined as the pattern of shared values, attitudes and norms held by the organization's (school's) members. Values were defined as explicit and/or implicit concepts of that which was considered to be good, right or preferred. Attitudes were generally defined as ways of thinking, acting or feeling. (Preferences, beliefs, opinions, sentiments, impressions, predispositions to act and positions taken by individuals or groups were considered to be attitudes.) Norms referred to group members' shared understandings about the organization's rules, rewards, events and traditions, heroes and legends, processes and expectations. Cultural strength of the organization (school) was interpreted using three measures:

1. The inferred proportion of group members who appeared to hold common values, attitudes and norms

2. The existence of informal rules that guided behaviour and the extent to which group members understood the organization's behavioural norms

3. The organization's value orientation with reference to Hodgkinson's (1978) value paradigm (Jones, 1991)

Semi-Structured Interviews

The literature reviews also indicated that the study of group values, attitudes and norms did not lend itself to the relatively rigid nature of printed questionnaires and statistical analysis. Instead, it was suggested that to understand school culture and to generate rich descriptions of it, it would be necessary to collect information and insights from within the school and to talk at length with its members to discover what they believed to be true and important. Consequently, studies of organizational culture tended to rely on naturalistic field research techniques, rather than traditional questionnaire-based studies.

Interview protocols were constructed with reference to other studies that had been conducted and the specific study research questions; however, the interviews were semi-structured. The purpose of the prepared questions was to provide a basic, consistent interview structure and to initiate investigation of aspects of school culture with respondents. Additional interview questions became apparent as data gathering was conducted. Clues and cues from the respondents guided the posing of new questions which resulted in a deeper appreciation of the schools' culture. The interview questions were designed to initiate discussions from which information about the three cultural aspects: values, attitudes and norms could be derived. To expand the scope of the discussions, responses to questions were sometimes followed by questions such as "Can you elaborate?" "What do you mean by that?" "Can you give some examples?" Following each printed question on the interview protocols, the cultural component the question was designed to address was indicated in parentheses; however, many responses provided information beyond the cultural component indicated.

Document Reviews

In addition to information gathering through interviewing, impressions were also formed informally through examination of documents such as staff and student handbooks, school brochures, newsletters and yearbooks and by observation throughout the schools.

Selection of High Performance Schools

Specific student academic achievement scores were used to identify the study's three high performance schools (although it must be noted that there are many important educational objectives of education systems other than academic achievement, such as various aspects of human, social and career development). At the time of this study, the B.C. Ministry of Education conducted province-wide assessments in mathematics, science, English reading and written expression and social studies. Each year, one of these subjects was selected for administration. At the secondary level, all Grade 10 students participated in the given year's assessment. The Ministry of Education also administered a high school exit examination program in which Grade 12 students were tested in 15 examinable subject areas.

For the purposes of this research, secondary school academic performance was measured (using Ministry of Education records) by computing the mean school scores for Grade 10 and Grade 12 students from the aforementioned assessments over a three-year period. On the basis of the mean scores, all public secondary and Group 2 private schools were rank-ordered. (Group 2 independent schools were those which, among other things, participated in provincial testing programs that included provincial learning assessments and Grade 12 provincial and scholarship examinations.) Once all schools were rank-ordered according to the standardized tests, the sum of the rankings was calculated for each school to derive the highest performing secondary schools.

The organizational cultures of three schools were studied to account for potential variations which may have been related to geographical location, community size and public and private school differences. Consequently, one school was selected from among the top performing urban, rural and Group 2 independent secondary school groups. For the purposes of this research, urban schools were located in municipalities with populations of 10,000 or more, and schools located in municipalities or unincorporated places with populations less than 10,000 were classified as rural. (The names of the participating schools were not publicly revealed to ensure anonymity.) The urban and independent schools were located in the Greater Vancouver area (part of the B.C. Lower Mainland); the rural school was located in the Regional District of East Kootenay in the B.C. interior (refer to Figure 4).

Figure 4 | British Columbia: Location of Study Schools

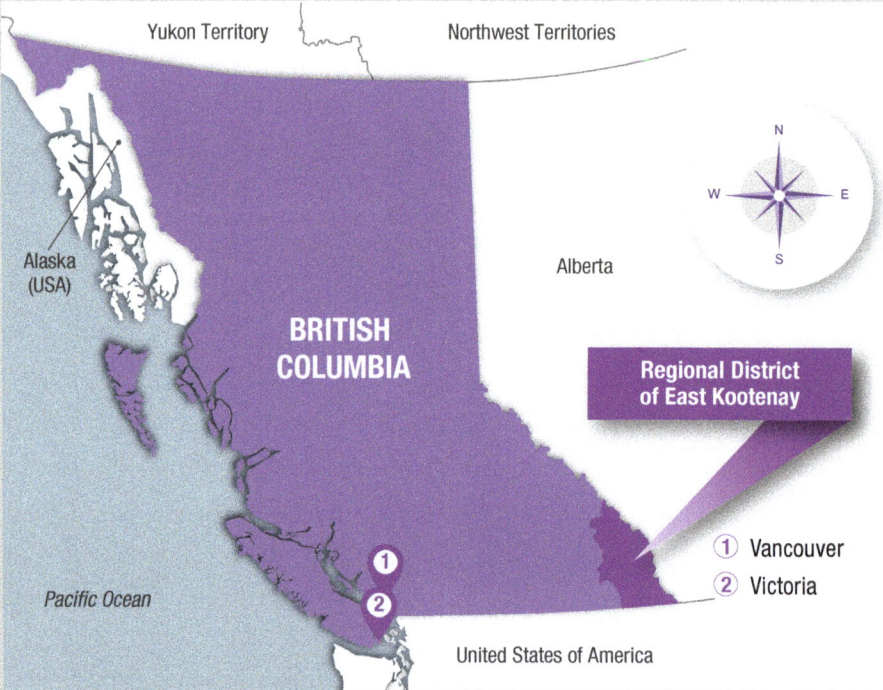

Pilot Testing

The draft interview protocols were pilot tested at Glenlyon-Norfolk School in Victoria, B.C. Based on the field-test responses, the interview questions were modified wherever they appeared to be redundant or where wording was inadequate.

Field Research

Semi-Structured Interviews

Data for the study were gathered primarily through the use of semi-structured, audio-taped interviews that were later transcribed. Interviews were conducted with all school administrators and random samples of students, teachers, parents and secretaries/custodians associated with each secondary school. On the basis of pilot test results, which indicated a high degree of homogeneity among interview responses, and in consideration of relative school size, it was decided that at the independent school, three administrators, five teachers, five students, five parents and one secretary/custodian would be interviewed; at the rural school, two administrators, five teachers, five students, five parents and one secretary/custodian would participate and at the urban school, three administrators, ten teachers, ten students, ten parents, and one secretary/custodian would be interviewed.

Sampling Procedures

Random sampling of teachers was conducted by first listing and sequentially numbering teachers, followed by the selection of either five or ten individuals (depending on school size) employing a random numbers table. Selection of students was conducted by initially listing and sequentially numbering students by grade level. Using a table of random numbers, either one or two students (depending on school size) were selected from each grade level. Parents to be included in the study were identified following the same procedure used for student selection. School secretaries and custodians were listed, sequentially numbered and one per school was randomly chosen. The random selection process worked satisfactorily; however, in the urban school, only seven randomly selected parents were available for interviewing. As a result, it became necessary to request three volunteers through the School Consultative Committee, a parent advisory group. Later analysis of randomly selected and volunteer parents' transcripts revealed no significant differences in the response patterns of the two groups.

Communication with School Community

Telephone and mail contact was made with the appropriate District Superintendents of Schools, as well as the Director of Independent Schools, to explain the nature of the research and to request the schools' involvement in the study. Upon receipt of such approval, similar contacts were made with school principals (or headmaster) to elicit their consent and support for the project and to identify an appropriate time period in which to conduct the research. Assurances were given that the name of the school and its members would not be made public in any way. Consent forms were signed by all participants prior to interviewing, and parents of student interviewees were asked to sign letters of permission. At the beginning of each interview, all respondents were informed of the general purposes of the interview, but care was taken not to reveal details of the specific research questions.

The study interviews were conducted over an approximately six-month period. Individual interviews ranged from thirty minutes to an hour in length, and approximately one week was spent at each of the three schools. In total, the audio-taped interviews generated over 1,000 pages of transcribed responses.

DATA CODING, ANALYSIS AND INTERPRETATION

Content analysis was used as the research methodology for analyzing the qualitative interview data. Each response was assigned a four-part code according to:

- the school type (I: independent, U: urban, and R: rural);
- response group and respondent number (e.g., S1: student 1, P1: parent 1, T1: teacher 1, SC1: secretary or custodian 1);
- cultural component(s) (N: norm, At: attitude, V1: value Type 1, V2A: value Type 2A, V2B: value Type 2B, V3: value Type 3) and
- the length of time at the school (number of years).

This coding system was based on the research definitions, purposes and questions.

Some interview data were assigned more than one code and therefore were placed in more than one category. Once information was sorted into categories, the data were further grouped into finer clusters that were given descriptive names (e.g., rules, rewards, heroes and legends) for use in the interpretive phase.

REPORTING

Following interpretation of the data and information, the research findings were combined in qualitative cultural summaries. The initial intent had been to provide a cultural summary for each of the schools' interview groups (students, parents, teachers, administrators and secretaries/custodians), and then for the school at large. However, a high degree of homogeneity was found to exist among the responses of all respondent groups within each school, and therefore, only the school-wide cultural summaries were reported. Results relating to each of the general study purposes and specific research questions were also reported descriptively.

For the purposes of this research, the cultural descriptions were independently adjudicated. Professor Alan Ryan, Department of Curriculum Studies, College of Education, University of Saskatchewan and Professor Fernand Gervais, Department of Educational Psychology, Faculty of Education, University of Regina (experts in qualitative, naturalistic inquiry) examined the cultural summaries and adjudicated their appropriateness with reference to the interview transcripts. The researcher also submitted the cultural summaries to representatives of the study's respondent groups at each school for validation. The university-based adjudicators found the cultural summaries to be accurate reflections of the interview transcripts. It was also the opinion of the school-based reviewers that the summaries captured the essence of the schools' cultures. The researcher considered all recommended modifications, which were few. Any errors in factual information were corrected; some language was modified to convey a more suitable tone and a few additional insights were incorporated where they were deemed appropriate. The two-year-long study culminated with the publication of a doctoral dissertation by Jones (1991).

SUMMARY

The case study of the organizational cultures of three high perfor-mance secondary schools in British Columbia reflects many of the standards of best practice as described in *The Program Evaluation Standards* and *Guiding Principles for Evaluators*. Several factors contributed to the successful completion of this project as follows:

- The study was conducted by a seasoned field researcher who paid close attention to the standards of best practice.

- The researcher carried out extensive literature research, which provided a solid foundation for the study, including its purpose, research questions and design.

- The study design proved to be effective in that sufficient data/information were gathered to answer all research questions.

- The adjudication and review processes, which involved ex-perts in naturalistic field research and members of the var-ious respondent groups, respectively, brought legitimacy to the report's cultural summaries (and ultimately the study's findings) and contributed to an atmosphere of openness and transparency.

- Communication was at the core of the entire study. Effective communication at the outset with district and school admin-istrators made it possible to obtain the cooperation of schools and members of their school communities in this project. Skill-ful and sensitive communication during the interview process itself was critically important in generating responses that would provide sufficient data/information to answer the re-search questions.

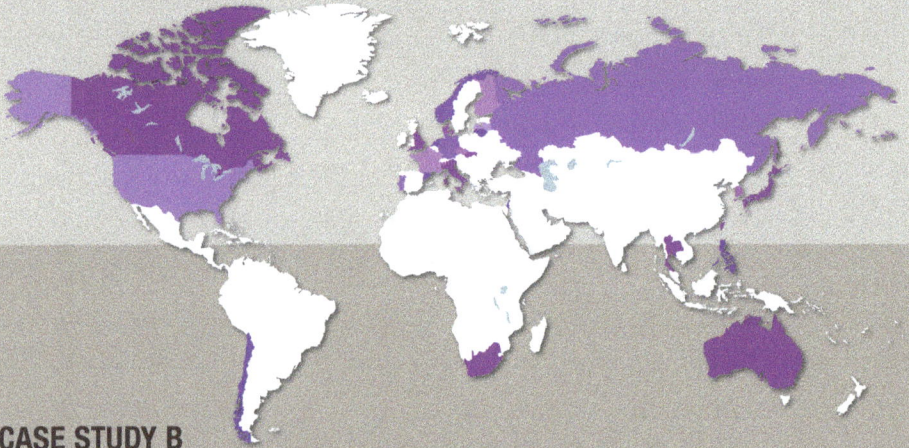

CASE STUDY B

CASE STUDY B
Second Information Technology in Education Study (SITES Module 2)

8

BACKGROUND AND CONTEXT OF THE STUDY

ICT in Education

In the decades leading up to this study (conducted during the period 1999 to 2002), computer and communication technologies developed rapidly, eventually converged, and the resulting information and communications technologies (ICT) became ubiquitous throughout society.

According to Kozma (2003), these technologies have the potential

> ❝ ...to make education and health care more widely available, foster cultural creativity and productivity, increase democratic participation and the responsiveness of governmental agencies, and enhance the social integration of individuals with different abilities and different cultural groups.
>
> ICT provides the tools needed by the knowledge economy and the information society. These tools allow us to create, collect, store, and use this new knowledge and information. They enable us to connect with people and resources all over the world, to collaborate in the creation of knowledge, and to distribute and benefit from knowledge products. (p. 2) ❞

The author explains that within this context, there was growing interest in the role(s) that ICT could play in improving education. For instance, new technologies have the potential to engage students and teachers by bringing real-world problems into the classroom, providing networking technologies to develop local and global communities to connect people with similar interests and providing a variety of tools to enhance student and teacher learning. In response to the potential of ICT for improving education, many countries have developed ICT-related policies to effect educational change.

The positive impacts of technology, however, are not distributed evenly across all groups and nations; this is known as the digital divide. For example, Pelgrum and Anderson (1999) reported that in 1998 there was approximately one computer for every nine lower secondary school students in Canada, but only one for every 133 students in Lithuania and only one for every 210 students in Cyprus.

Furthermore, there are disparities within countries related to social and economic factors.

Although ICT holds great promise for education, it is not, in and of itself, a panacea. Positive impacts of ICT will not result automatically from its presence in the classroom; how teachers use ICT is of paramount importance. Although increasingly educators, schools and education systems are integrating ICT into the learning process, some schools and teachers remain locked in the traditional paradigm in which limited use is made of ICT. At the time of this study, there was evidence that, within each of the countries involved, at least some innovative teachers were integrating ICT into their teaching. These innovations were the focus of the study.

SITES Modules

The Second Information Technology in Education Study (SITES) was a project authorized by the International Association for the Evaluation of Educational Achievement (IEA). The study was conducted in three modules.

Module 1 (1997-1999) involved a survey of principals and school technology coordinators in a sample of schools in 26 countries. The study examined the extent to which the following were available or existed in the schools:

- A supportive climate for the use of ICT
- The ICT infrastructure (e.g., hardware, software, Internet access)
- Staff development and support services related to ICT
- The adoption of objectives and practices that reflected autonomous learning strategies

Module 3 (2002-2006) involved a follow-up survey of principals and school technology coordinators, as well as a survey of teachers and students. The study also included an assessment of students' use of ICT skills to solve mathematics and science problems.

Module 2 (1999-2002), described in this chapter, was a comprehensive examination of the relationship between ICT use and innovative pedagogical practices in primary, lower secondary and upper secondary school classrooms. The study was primarily qualitative in nature and relied on a case study approach. Twenty-eight countries participated in the project from North and South America, Europe, Asia and Africa (refer to Figure 5).

PURPOSE OF THE STUDY

According to Kozma (2003), the goals of SITES 2 were as follows:

- Identify and provide rich descriptions for innovations that are considered valuable by each country and that might be considered for large-scale implementation or adoption by schools in other countries

- Provide information to national and local policy makers that they can use to make decisions related to ICT and the role it might play in advancing their country's education goals and addressing educational needs and problems

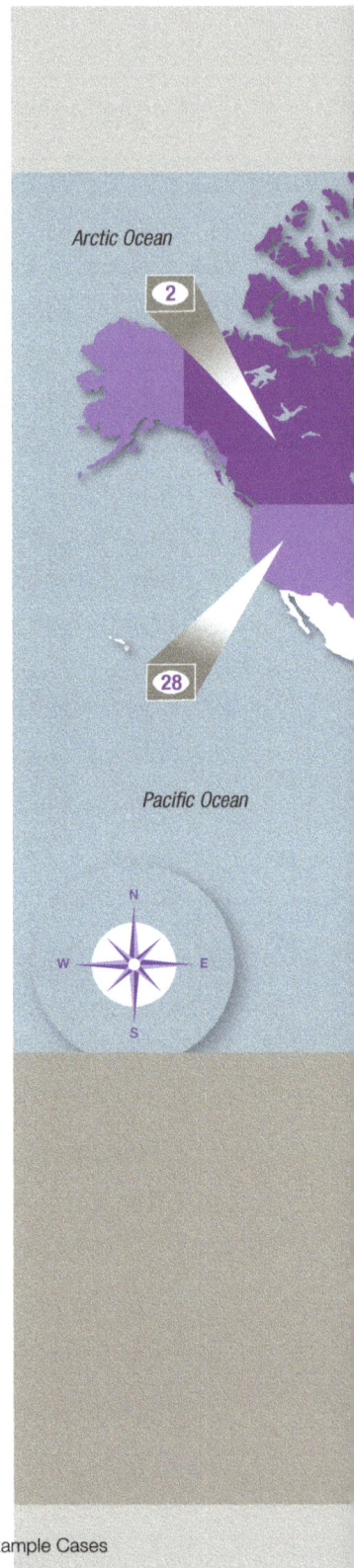

Arctic Ocean

Pacific Ocean

Figure 5 | SITES Module 2: Participating Countries

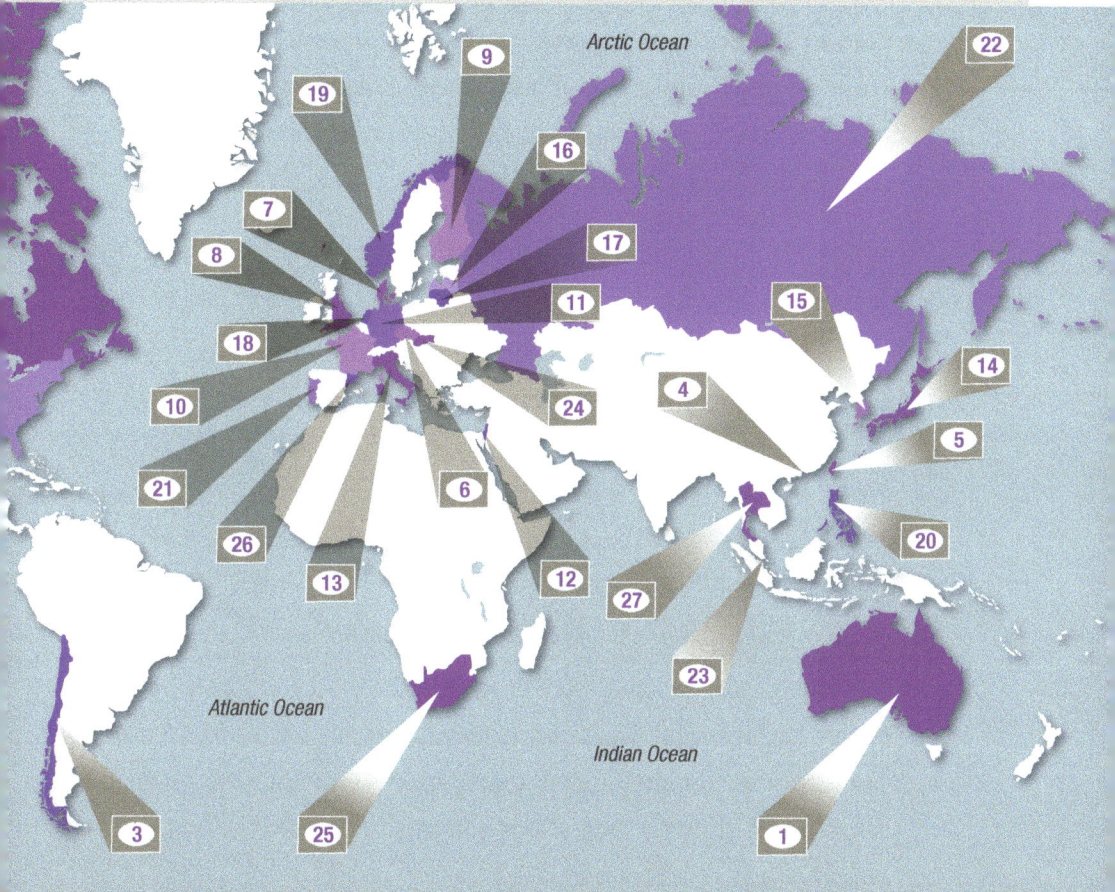

1	Australia	11	Germany	21	Portugal

1 Australia
2 Canada
3 Chile
4 China Hong Kong
5 Chinese Taipei
6 Czech Republic
7 Denmark
8 England
9 Finland
10 France

11 Germany
12 Israel
13 Italy
14 Japan
15 South Korea
16 Latvia
17 Lithuania
18 The Netherlands
19 Norway
20 Philippines

21 Portugal
22 Russia
23 Singapore
24 Slovakia
25 South Africa
26 Spain, Catalonia
27 Thailand
28 United States of America

- Provide teachers and other practitioners with new ideas about how they can use ICT to improve classroom practices
- Add to the body of research knowledge and theory about the contexts and factors, within and across countries, that contribute to the successful and sustained use of innovative technology-based pedagogical practices

RESEARCH QUESTIONS

The following research questions, organized by four topics of interest, formed the foundation of the study design:

ICT and Innovative Classroom Practices

✔ What are the ICT-based pedagogical practices that countries consider to be innovative? How are these innovative practices similar and different from one country to another?

✔ What new teacher and student roles are associated with innovative pedagogical practices using technology? How are these innovations changing what teachers and students do in the classroom? How do they affect patterns of teacher-student and student-student interactions?

✔ How do these practices change the classroom? In what ways does the use of ICT change the organization of the classroom, extend the school day, break down the walls of the classroom and involve other actors (e.g., parents, scientists or business people) in the learning process?

✔ What capabilities of the applied technologies support innovative pedagogical practices? How do these capabilities shape the practices they support?

ICT and the Curriculum

✔ How do these practices change curriculum content and goals? What impact do these practices have on student competencies, attitudes and other outcomes? Have they changed what students are learning and what teachers need to learn? Have they changed the ways student outcomes are assessed?

ICT in the Schools

✔ What contextual factors are associated with the use of these innovations? Which factors seem to be present across different innovative pedagogical practices? Which ones are associated with different practices? What are the implications of contextual factors for the sustainability and transferability of these innovations?

✔ What are the barriers to using ICT in these innovative ways? How are teachers overcoming these barriers? How do they cope with limited resources?

ICT Policies

✔ Which local policies related to staff development, student computer fees, facilities access, technical support and other issues appear to be effective in supporting these innovations?

✔ Which national telecommunications policies related to such things as school Internet access, equipment purchase, teacher training and student Internet use seem to be effective in supporting these innovations?

THE STUDY TEAM

The study was led by an international team of researchers that formed the International Coordinating Center (ICC) located at the Center for Technology in Learning at Stanford Research Institute (SRI) International in Menlo Park, California. The project director was an emeritus principal scientist and Fulbright senior specialist at the Center for Technology in Learning at SRI International. Other members of the study team included

- a research social scientist in SRI International's Center for Educational Policy;
- a professor of education and founding director of the Institute for Research on Learning Technologies at York University in Toronto;
- the project manager for National, International and Special Projects with the Education Quality and Accountability Office (EQAO) in Toronto and
- an associate professor at the Faculty of Educational Science and Technology and a senior researcher at the Center for Applied Educational Research at the University of Twente in The Netherlands.

The study team received advice and guidance from a six-person SITES International Steering Committee (ISC) of assessment, research and educational technology experts from the United States, The Netherlands, Hong Kong, Norway and Japan.

The National Research Coordinators (NRCs) from the 28 participating countries were involved in all aspects of the study, including project design, instrument development, data collection and analysis, as well as report writing. It was the NRCs who led research efforts within their own countries.

EVALUATION METHODOLOGY

Procedures and Guidelines

One challenge of this comparative international study was to find a balance between the need for standardization and the need to accommodate local/country contexts and needs. To this end, the ICC collaborated with NRCs to establish a common set of study procedures, instruments and guidelines. The result was a researcher's handbook that was distributed to NRCs in print form and was also posted electronically on the project's Web site. The handbook was periodically revised as needed.

Case selection was critical to the success of the project. The study's focus was on innovative pedagogical practices in the classroom; however, it was recognized that innovations of interest to the project could involve multiple classrooms or could include activities outside of the classroom or school provided the remote activities were coordinated in the classroom. Whereas random sampling is a feature of quantitative studies where representativeness to a population is important, the selection of cases in a qualitative study can be purposeful to meet the needs of the study. As Kozma (2003) explains:

> In SITES Module 2, the cases were not meant to represent "typical" classroom practices but those that were "innovative." The selected cases were intended to represent the aspirations of each country rather than represent what was going on in many classrooms. Our goal was to identify the kinds of ICT-enabled practices that each country valued and wanted to hold up to others in their country and to the world. Consequently, it was important that the selection process be credible and the selected cases be highly compelling. (p. 25)

A high-level summary of the international criteria for case selection was as follows:

- The innovation should show evidence of significant changes in the roles for teachers and students, the curriculum goals, assessment practices and/or education materials or infrastructure.
- Technology must play a substantial role and provide added value to pedagogical practice.
- There was a preference that there would be evidence that the innovation was associated with positive student outcomes.
- The innovation should show potential to be sustainable and transferable.
- The practice must be innovative as locally defined.

To assist in the process of selecting credible cases, the NRC in each country established a national panel made up of representatives of educational technology organizations, primary and/or secondary teachers, school and/or school board administrators, education researchers with experience in this field and ministries of education. The panel members became familiar with the case-selection criteria, developed a selection process in collaboration with the NRC, proposed potential cases for consideration, selected the cases and provided the NRC with support and advice on conducting the case studies and developing case reports. To keep the number of cases manageable, the decision was taken to limit the number for each country to no more than 12 for the international study: a maximum of four from each of primary, lower secondary and upper secondary school. Countries could choose to conduct more case studies for their own use. At the conclusion of the study, 174 case reports were received from NRCs. The number of cases ranged from one (Japan) to 12 (Germany). The average was approximately six cases per country.

Instruments

As was previously mentioned, SITES 2 used case studies to address the project's purposes and to answer the specific research questions. Both qualitative information and quantitative data were collected; however, the project was predominantly qualitative. The following instruments and sources of data were included (Kozma, 2003):

- Interviews with school administrators, technology coordinators and innovative teachers
- Focus group discussions with other teachers not involved in the innovation, students, parents and other community members
- A principal and school technology coordinator survey, including selected items from SITES Module 1
- Classroom observations that derived information such as teacher and student behaviours, seating arrangements and resource allocation
- Documents and/or archival data such as project proposals, curriculum materials, teacher-developed lesson plans, instructional material and student-generated products of various kinds

The ICC members pilot tested these instruments in one case from each of their respective countries: the United States, Canada and The Netherlands. For each case, it took two researchers about one week to collect the data. The ICC shared their experiences with the NRCs, adjustments were made to the instruments as required and administration protocols were developed. Subsequently, field tests were administered in 17 countries, and the instruments and protocols were revised yet again. The final instruments and protocols were translated into the various languages by the NRCs and were used to gather data on the selected case studies.

Case Reports

In anticipation of a large number of cases, and because the ICC alone was responsible for cross-case analysis, it was decided that a standard format would be developed for the case reports. In consultation with the NRCs, it was decided that case write-ups would combine two approaches: a narrative approach in which structured prose write-ups were organized according to the study's purposes and research questions and a data-matrix approach using "slot filling," similarly organized around the study's conceptual framework, and calling for short answers to a series of questions describing the case and presenting evidence relative to specific aspects of the framework. Case report guidelines contained suggested word limits for a standard set of sections and called for a 10-page narrative. In addition to the narrative for each case, NRCs were to submit glossaries of any special terms used and the portion of the data matrix pertaining to classroom practice (Kozma, 2003). Case report guidelines, which described a two-stage process for report writing, were pilot and field tested in conjunction with instrument development and were developed in consultation with the NRCs.

Quality Monitoring

An important function of the ICC was to monitor the quality of research that was conducted in all 28 participating countries. This was accomplished in the following five ways:

- The ICC monitored the processes of national panel selection and the choice of cases for study in each country.
- The ICC mapped the data- and information-gathering instruments and guidelines to the project framework and specific research questions.

- The ICC conducted workshops with the NRCs on data and information gathering, as well as data analysis to ensure consistent application of the techniques.

- The case report guidelines and templates were structured to, as much as possible, ensure comprehensive and standardized presentation of findings that were supported by evidence.

- The NRCs submitted their first case write-ups to the ICC and another NRC (a friendly critic) for review with reference to the reporting guidelines. Feedback was provided on the degree of adherence to the reporting guidelines, comprehensiveness of the presentation, potential bias and substantiation of assertions.

Apart from periodic meetings of the ICC and NRCs, strong communication was fostered through the use of conference calls and particularly the project Web site, which was used extensively for information sharing.

DATA CODING, ANALYSIS AND INTERPRETATION

A mixed research model, combining qualitative and quantitative approaches, was used in this study. In the words of Kozma (2003):

> The goal of our analysis of the cases was to understand innovative pedagogical practices using technology, how these innovations changed what it is that teachers and students do, the roles ICT plays in supporting them, and how the innovations are associated with various outcomes and contextual conditions. The mixed model is both necessitated by and takes advantage of the fact that we had 174 case studies to analyze. (p. 35)

As a first step in the analysis, the ICC developed a cover sheet to characterize each of the cases. The cover sheet consisted of a 27-item scheme that was directly linked to the study framework and research questions and included variables such as

- grade and subject area;
- description of the innovation;
- contextual factors associated with the innovation;
- resulting curriculum changes;
- teacher and student classroom activities;
- types of technology used and
- reported impact of the innovation.

The ICC also developed a set of guidelines that elaborated on the meaning of the coding system, so that all ICC members would consistently code the statements made in the case reports that were supported by evidence from the data. Each of the 174 case reports was read and coded by one of the ICC members with reference to the coding scheme. To ensure reliability and to validate the coding, the ICC shared the coding for each case, together with any questions for clarification, with the respective NRC.

Step two of the analysis involved looking for patterns within cases. Kozma (2003) states:

> Our goal in this analysis was to find coordinated practices that meaningfully distinguished one set of cases from others. Such patterns might allow us to understand how certain teaching practices fit together with certain activities by students using technology, and how these practices might differ from one set of cases to another. (p. 48)

Consequently, the ICC performed a cluster analysis (k-means clustering, a SAS FASTCLUS procedure) as an efficient way of examining patterns within this large data set. Seven clusters emerged from the analysis (Tool Use, Student Collaborative Research, Information Management, Teacher Collaboration, Outside Communication, Product Creation and Tutorial).

The third step in the analysis was the examination of a subset of cases to attain a better understanding of the meaning of the clusters and how the corresponding innovative practices looked in the classroom. The ICC did not have the resources to conduct this detailed analysis of all 174 cases, so the output of the cluster analysis aided the team in identifying cases for more in-depth study. The cluster analysis listed all cases in order of their proximity to the centre of the cluster (the centroid). Those cases closest to the centroid were considered to typify the cluster. Forty-seven cases were selected across the seven clusters, including cases from all participating countries with the exception of one.

A detailed coding scheme, closely tied to the conceptual framework and research questions, was used to characterize practices across the 47 country cases. The coding scheme was used in conjunction with ATLAS ti, a software package to facilitate qualitative analysis. For the purpose of this analysis, the primary focus of the coding was related to the practices of teachers and students and their use of ICT.

REPORTING

At the conclusion of the three-year study, a book titled *Technology, Innovation, and Educational Change: A Global Perspective* (Kozma, 2003) was published by the International Society for Technology in Education (ISTE) and served as the project's final report. The book, which contained chapters by each of the ICC members, included the following topics:

- The global phenomenon of ICT and educational change
- Study procedures
- ICT and innovative classroom practices
- ICT and the curriculum
- School context, sustainability and transferability of innovations
- Local and national ICT policies
- Stellar cases of technology-supported pedagogical innovations
- Summary and implications for ICT-based educational change

SUMMARY

The case study research approach was well-suited to the goals and research questions of SITES Module 2, which focused on describing innovative pedagogical practices in education and the context within which they occurred. This large-scale multinational comparative project reflected many of the professional standards and principles of program evaluation as follows:

- The project involved highly experienced professionals. The study, authorized by IEA, was supervised by an ICC, the members of which were experts in education policy and the innovative use of technology for teaching and learning, and conducting large-scale international comparative studies, case studies and program evaluations. An ISC, the members of which had global reputations in the field, provided invaluable advice and guidance to the ICC. In addition, the NRCs from each of the participating countries brought their knowledge and experience in research, assessment and evaluation to the table.

- The ICC, in collaboration with its partners, established the framework for the study (including its goals/purposes and research questions) and all aspects of the work plan. Effective project management strategies were required to ensure successful completion of this complex international project.

- Extensive research on ICT and educational change was conducted prior to the study and helped to shape its framework.

- A comprehensive understanding of the contextual elements of the countries' cases emerged during the course of the research project.

- All project partners made every effort to ensure country/cultural needs and sensitivities were addressed. NRCs, in collaboration with the ICC and the countries' national panels, were instrumental in making this happen.

- There was effective communication at all levels (e.g., between IEA and both the ISC and the ICC, the ISC and the ICC, the ICC and NRCs, NRCs and their respective national panels, and among ICC members).

- The evaluation methodologies employed were successful in generating the data and information required to address the study's purposes and research questions. The published book (the final project report) provided a unique source of information about innovative pedagogical practices using ICT and was a valuable resource for education policy, practice and research.

- The study was conducted within the agreed-upon time frame (1999-2002), and the book was published, as planned, one year later.

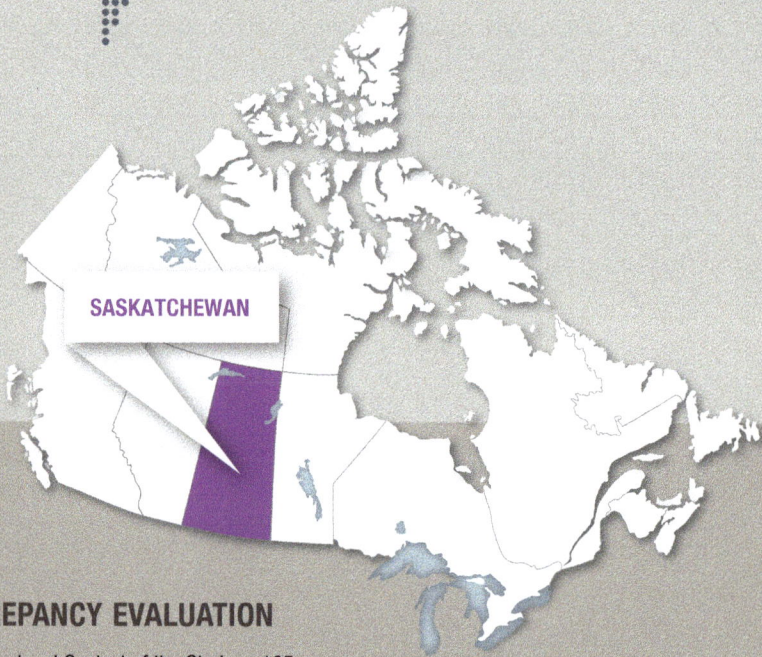

DISCREPANCY EVALUATION

DISCREPANCY EVALUATION

Evaluation of the Indian and Métis Education Staff Development Program

BACKGROUND AND CONTEXT OF THE STUDY

Historical Context

Over the years, there have been many changes in policies and approaches to Indian and Métis Education in Saskatchewan, involving a variety of agencies and levels of government.

Saskatchewan became a province of Canada in 1905, and for four decades, the federal government assumed responsibility for Saskatchewan Indian education. During that time, various governments experimented with different strategies for educating Indian children, including school types, curriculum content and instructional approaches. In 1944, the province took over responsibility for the education of Métis and Non-Status Indians. Prior to 1960, assimilation of Indian and Métis children into mainstream society was the primary educational goal, which meant they were expected to abandon their traditional lifestyle, including their homes, native languages and values: in reality, their cultures.

In the 1960s, federal and provincial education officials came to the realization that the approaches they had been using for Indian and Métis education were not working, and that new approaches were required. At that time, there was a growing awareness that culture was fundamental to the person, and that acceptance of one's culture was an important element of successful education. Consequently, in the 1960s and beyond, many changes were made to reflect the new philosophy concerning Indian and Métis education, including adaptations to curricula, teacher training and recruitment and ongoing teacher education workshops.

During the 1970s, a new model evolved which encouraged local initiatives and partnerships. Curriculum materials and resources were developed by the Saskatchewan Indian Cultural College, the Department of Northern Saskatchewan, local school boards, school staffs and individual teachers. Also in the 1970s, the first education training program for Indian peoples: the Indian Teacher Education Program, was established, as well as the Northern Teacher Education Program.

The 1980s was a period which saw major changes in Saskatchewan's public education system. A public enquiry – a rethinking of education – gave rise to the *Directions* report (1984), which made numerous recommendations to improve education in the province, including the implementation of a new *Core Curriculum*. Also during this time, several reports were prepared which made recommendations regarding Indian and Métis education.

Whereas in the past, Indian and Métis children had predominantly attended northern, rural or reserve schools, they were beginning to attend urban schools in ever-increasing numbers, which meant that more and more, urban school boards were requiring help with meeting the needs of these students. As a result, the provincial government created the Community Education Branch (which later became the Indian and Métis Education Unit) of the Department of Education. The mandate of the Unit was to

- identify and develop appropriate curriculum resource materials;
- integrate Indian and Métis content and perspectives into all provincial curricula and
- oversee the establishment of community schools.

During this time, the Department also established the Native Curriculum Review Committee and the Indian and Métis Curriculum Advisory Committee (which was succeeded by the Indian and Métis Education Advisory Committee [IMEAC]) to provide advice on matters related to Indian and Métis education. In the same time period, Indian and Métis organizations created educational institutions and programs as follows:

- The Federation of Saskatchewan Indian Nations established the Saskatchewan Indian Cultural Centre in Saskatoon and the Saskatchewan Indian Federated College at the University of Regina.
- The Association of Métis and Non-Status Indians of Saskatchewan (which subsequently became the Métis Nation of Saskatchewan) established the Gabriel Dumont Institute of Native Studies and Applied Research.
- The Gabriel Dumont Institute developed the Saskatchewan Urban Native Teacher Education Program (SUNTEP) to provide specialized teacher education training to assist teacher candidates to acquire the knowledge and skills to be responsive to the needs of Native students in urban centres with locations (at that time) in Regina, Saskatoon and Prince Albert (refer to Figure 6).

Figure 6 | Saskatchewan: Location of Major Urban Centres

Northwest Territories

Nunavut

Hudson Bay

Alberta

Manitoba

SASKATCHEWAN

③

②

Ontario

①

N

W · E

S

United States of America

Urban centres:

① Regina ② Saskatoon ③ Prince Albert

The curriculum reforms of the 1980s continued into the 1990s, with the Indian and Métis Education Unit and IMEAC playing important roles in ensuring that Indian and Métis content and perspectives were incorporated into the *Core Curriculum* to be used with all students of the province. The Indian and Métis Education Staff Development Program evolved from the collaboration of the Indian and Métis Education Unit of Saskatchewan Education and IMEAC.

The Staff Development Program

Following the *Directions* report (1984), a Five Year Action Plan for Native Curriculum Development was established with the following main objectives:

- All students and teachers in provincial schools were expected to develop an appreciation of the political, cultural, socioeconomic and historical context of North American Native peoples.

- Teachers were expected to become sensitive to Native and northern issues, and curriculum materials, resources and programs were expected to be relevant to Native and northern students.

- School curricula and educational institutions were expected to convey positive and accurate information to support Native students in developing a positive self-image and cultural identity.

An Indian and Métis Awareness In-service Program was implemented during the 1984-1985 school year. Local teacher leaders, supported by resource people contracted by the Department of Education, delivered professional development workshops to educators to raise awareness about North American Indian and Métis peoples and provide guidance in developing and delivering cross-cultural instructional strategies. During the 1989-1990 school year, the Awareness In-service Program was replaced by the Indian and Métis Education Staff Development Program, which provided a new delivery model.

Whereas the Awareness Program had been delivered regionally by lead teachers, the Staff Development Program involved consultants from Saskatchewan Education working with school community teams. This approach meant that there was local control and responsibility for integrating the content areas into the school and community at large.

The general purpose of the program was to prepare the leadership of the school community to develop and implement programs to address issues in Indian and Métis education. The program was designed to give schools the tools to effect positive changes that would benefit all students in the province. The objectives of the Indian and Métis Education Staff Development Program were to assist participants to

- identify issues in Indian and Métis education to address in the local community;
- develop, implement and evaluate plans to address the needs identified in the local community;
- develop and enhance team building and cooperative learning skills and
- network with others involved in the program.

The Staff Development Program's resource binder contained detailed information on the following broad topics:

- Indian and Métis awareness
- Developing Indian and Métis participation
- Cross-cultural education
- Cultural and racial awareness
- Materials evaluation
- Instructional methods and strategies
- Framework and processes for effective staff development, team building and planning for change

The Indian and Métis Education Staff Development Program had three principal components:

1 | a seminar,
2 | resources and
3 | networking meetings.

In year one, teams comprising one school division central office member, one school administrator, one teacher, and two members of the community participated in a three-day summer seminar during which time they were provided with resources, information and activities associated with the various topics contained in the resource binder. Following the workshop, the local teams were expected to work closely with the consultants from the Indian and Métis Education Unit. In years two and three, it was expected that the local teams would develop experience and become more self-sufficient, thereby requiring increasingly less of the Department consultants' time. The program, as mentioned before, also included annual networking meetings to share experiences and to provide supports to school community teams. Schools were charged a participation fee to attend the meetings and were responsible for their own members' travel-related expenses.

PURPOSE OF THE STUDY

The Saskatchewan Department of Education understood the importance of evaluation in all aspects of education including curriculum and instruction, program design and implementation, as well as all planned educational activities. Consequently, Department policy established the expectation that the progress of all programs and initiatives would be evaluated in conjunction with the agencies/organizations involved. From the time the Staff Development Program was designed and implemented there was an intention to evaluate the program and make revisions based on feedback from the school community teams and IMEAC. It was also recognized that as the program evolved, other needs were likely to emerge and be incorporated into the program.

The Indian and Métis Education Staff Development Program had been operating for three years in a pilot phase. Acting on a recommendation from IMEAC, the Indian and Métis Education Unit requested that the Department's Assessment and Evaluation Unit conduct an evaluation of the program. Although no particular evaluation approach was advocated for program evaluation, discrepancy evaluation seemed best suited for this study, because the evaluation was of a pilot initiative and was meant to be formative in nature with a focus on program improvement. The general purpose of the evaluation was to provide information to the Indian and Métis Education Unit, IMEAC and other stakeholders concerning the effectiveness of the program.

RESEARCH QUESTIONS

The following general issues and related research questions formed the foundation of the evaluation study design:

Issue: Objectives of the Program

✔ To what extent are the program's objectives understood by team members?

✔ Are there any changes needed to the program's objectives?

Issue: Value of the Program's Components

✔ To what extent do team members feel the three main components: seminar, resources and networking meetings support the delivery of the program?

✔ To what extent do team members feel logistics such as facilities, fees and timetabling support the delivery of the program?

Issue: Effectiveness of the Program

✔ To what extent have the intended objectives of the program been realized?

✔ Are there any unintended outcomes (positive or negative) of the program?

Issue: Emerging Needs of the Program

✔ Are there additional issues or areas of concern that the program should address?

✔ In what ways can the program be improved?

THE STUDY TEAM

The evaluation was conducted by two experienced program evaluators from the Assessment and Evaluation Unit of Saskatchewan Education.

EVALUATION METHODOLOGY

Preliminary Meetings

Prior to any consideration of project design, the study team met with members of the Indian and Métis Education Unit to clarify the direction and focus of the evaluation and develop the research questions. As a result of the consultations, it was agreed that the study team would operate independently of the Indian and Métis Education Unit, and decisions were made concerning the purposes and audiences of the evaluation, the intended uses of the study's findings and the timeframe of the evaluation (approximately twelve months).

Data-Gathering Methods

Data and information for the evaluation study were gathered through the use of document analysis, a questionnaire, a telephone survey, on-site visits and group interviews.

Document Analysis

An analysis of Department documents was undertaken during a one-month period to gain an understanding of the historical context of the study, gather background information for the development of research issues and questions and obtain a description of the Indian and Métis Education Staff Development Program. An evaluation proposal was then submitted to the Indian and Métis Education Unit and IMEAC for their review and approval. Analyses of year-end reports prepared by schools participating in the Staff Development Program, as well as reports of annual evaluations conducted by the Indian and Métis Education Unit were undertaken to provide information to support the development of the questionnaire and questions for use in the group interviews.

Questionnaire

The questionnaire, which was designed to collect information related to the research issues and questions, was to be completed by the members of all school community teams that participated in the Staff Development Program. Following validation of the draft questionnaire by the Indian and Métis Education Unit and IMEAC, the survey was pilot tested with approximately 20 individuals attending a networking meeting. The responses to the questionnaire and subsequent discussions with respondents provided the study team with information that led to revisions to the survey instrument. Furthermore, data and information gathered from the pilot test were analyzed, and statistics were generated to determine how the data and information could be summarized and displayed in the final report.

The Indian and Métis Education Unit mailed the questionnaires to school community teams, and they were given approximately one month to respond. Of the 200 questionnaires that were distributed, 44 (or 22 percent) were returned. The study team had concerns about the relatively low response rate, and so a follow-up telephone survey was conducted with a 10 percent random sample of non-respondents. The results of the follow-up survey indicated that there were no significant differences in the response patterns of respondents and non-respondents to the initial survey. As a result, the study team felt confident in the data and information derived from the mail-out questionnaire.

Telephone Survey

A telephone survey was conducted with a random sample of 100 school principals and 22 Directors of Education whose schools/ divisions had not yet participated in the Staff Development Program. The survey, which contained questions related to the demographic make-up of the schools/school divisions, their awareness of the Staff Development Program, the reasons why they had not yet taken part and other ways the school/division may have been addressing similar needs, was conducted over a two-month period. Prior to carrying out the telephone survey, it was pilot tested with ten school- and five school-division-based administrators to ensure the questions were clear, concise and effective in generating the required data and information.

On-Site Visits

During a four-month period, the study team conducted on-site visits where the Indian and Métis Education Staff Development Program had been implemented. Anticipating possible variation by geographic location, a purposeful sample of one urban and one remote rural school community was selected in consultation with the Indian and Métis Education Unit. The purpose of the visits was to provide the study team with an authentic, first-hand appreciation of staff development programs in the context of community life. In other words, the visits would "give life" to the data and information gathered by means of the earlier questionnaire. Using the questionnaire data, the study team developed questions pertaining to the two school communities' Staff Development Programs, including the schools' background/context, resources (internal and external to the school) and various school community activities. The team also had an opportunity to tour the schools and speak with key community leaders and members. In both the urban and rural communities, prior to conducting the site visits, the study team met with community leaders and interested members to explain the purposes of the visits and to assure them that all measures would be taken to ensure the confidentiality of information gathered and the anonymity of the local school community. The qualitative information obtained through the on-site visits complemented the statistical data generated by the questionnaire and telephone surveys.

Group Interviews

Following the on-site visits, the data and information from all data-gathering methods were used to produce further questions to pursue during group interviews which were held during an ensuing networking meeting of school community teams participating in the

Staff Development Program. The semi-structured interviews were conducted with groups of six to eight people and covered topics that were linked to the research questions and related issues.

DATA CODING, ANALYSIS AND INTERPRETATION

As the questionnaires were returned to the Assessment and Evaluation Unit, and as data and information from the telephone survey, on-site visits and group interviews became available, the study team, employing content analysis, began to code responses to open-ended questions. For the most part, data were summarized by descriptive statistics such as frequency counts, percentages and means, as well as descriptive, qualitative summaries. The study team interpreted the data in consultation with the Indian and Métis Education Unit and IMEAC.

REPORTING

Approximately one year after the evaluation study was initiated, the study team submitted a draft report to the Indian and Métis Education Unit and IMEAC for feedback. Following minor adjustments (based on the feedback) the final report was distributed to the Indian and Métis Education Unit of the Department of Education, IMEAC, each team participating in the Staff Development Program, the provincial education stakeholder groups and all Canadian provincial ministries of education. In addition, an executive summary report was prepared and provided to all Directors of Education and school principals in the province, as well as all school community team members who participated in the program.

SUMMARY

Discrepancy evaluation proved to be a useful approach for conducting the evaluation of the Indian and Métis Education Staff Development Program pilot initiative. Standards/expectations for the various components of the program had been established; the performance/outcomes related to standards/expectations were examined for evidence of congruency or discrepancy; reasons for any discrepancies were determined and possible corrective actions/program enhancements were recommended.

Many of *The Program Evaluation Standards* and *Guiding Principles for Evaluators* are evident in the description of the evaluation methodology as follows:

- The evaluation was conducted by a qualified, experienced two-person team which had not only conducted many previous program evaluations, but had also provided instruction (by way of program evaluation workshops) to a variety of education- and non-education-related professionals.

- The study team, in conjunction with the client organizations, established the framework (including the study purposes, objects of the evaluation and research questions), roles of various stakeholder groups and work plan for the study, which incorporated effective project management strategies.

- Prior to conducting the evaluation, the study team developed a comprehensive understanding of the contextual elements of the evaluation and considered them in developing the study design.

- Evaluation procedures were practical for the identified purposes and allowed for the generation of appropriate data and information to answer the research questions.

- The evaluators, in consultation with the clients and stakeholders, made every effort to ensure that cultural sensitivities were addressed at all stages of the evaluation; respect for everyone involved was a key foundational principle of the study.

- Confidentiality of individual participants' contributions to the study was safeguarded as was the anonymity of the local school communities involved.

- Communication was a key component of the study, including preliminary meetings with clients and ongoing consultations with them, information exchanges with school division and school administrators and ongoing interactions with the school communities. Good communication ensured acceptance of the value of the study and provided for an air of openness and transparency.

- The final reports (including the executive summary report) were submitted within the agreed-upon timeframe, contained all relevant and appropriate information, were presented in a clear, straightforward and non-biased fashion and met the needs of the client organizations and all stakeholder groups.

SASKATCHEWAN

EVALUATION FOR
DECISION MAKING

EVALUATION FOR DECISION MAKING

10

Evaluation of the Scenic Valley School Division Program for Protected Classroom Instruction

BACKGROUND AND CONTEXT OF THE STUDY

Responsibility for Education in Canada

Canada is a confederation of ten provinces and three territories. Areas of responsibility are divided between the federal and provincial/territorial governments. The federal government is responsible for portfolios such as national defence, external affairs, fisheries, transportation (shipping and railways), telecommunications, energy and the banking and monetary systems. The provinces and territories are responsible for areas such as health, forestry, highways and education; there is no federal department of education.

Consequently, each Canadian jurisdiction establishes its own policies related to curriculum, teacher certification, school accreditation and reporting of student learning progress. School boards (in some jurisdictions they are called school districts or school divisions) set their local policies within the larger framework of policies established by the provincial/territorial ministries of education. School board responsibilities include hiring and supervising of personnel; acquiring and maintaining school buildings and facilities; delivering education programs and developing local policies and programs to meet the needs of staff, students, parents and the community (Jones, 2003).

Scenic Valley School Division

Scenic Valley School Division was located in a rural, agricultural area northeast of the city of Regina, Saskatchewan. In 1994, four small school divisions (Balcarres, Grenfell, Wolseley and Valleyview) amalgamated to create the Scenic Valley School Division. The total population in the area served by the School Division was approximately 12,000, about 17 percent of whom were First Nations people. The School Division employed 87 full-time equivalent teachers (95 individuals), and its seven schools enrolled a total of 1,349 students. The School Division had no history of or experience with administering commercial, standardized student achievement tests.

Program for Protected Classroom Instruction

In 1996, the Saskatchewan Department of Education approved a four-day instructional week initiative in the Scenic Valley School Division on a trial/pilot basis. The following year, the pilot was extended through to the year 2000. The primary rationale given for the four-day school week model was to reduce school operating costs (e.g., energy, busing of students, maintaining school facilities) while safeguarding classroom instructional time. To demonstrate its commitment to the principle of not sacrificing instructional time in the four-day model, the School Division called the initiative the Program for Protected Classroom Instruction. In this model, all of the schools operated on a 197-day school calendar comprised of 163 "longer instructional" days (5.4 hours) and 34 "regular non-instructional" days (5.0 hours). Whereas the four-day instructional week applied to students, the "regular non-instructional" days (usually Fridays) were used by teachers for activities such as administrative duties, instructional preparation, collaboration, parent-teacher meetings, professional development and staff meetings. It was the responsibility of the school principals to decide how to add the extra 24 minutes during the "longer instructional" school days (e.g., starting the school day earlier, reducing the length of lunch breaks). In each week, the four "longer instructional" days were intended to be used almost exclusively for instruction, which was to be protected from interruption as much as possible by

- not allowing early classroom dismissals for teacher or student special events;
- keeping interruptions to the classroom routine to a minimum (e.g., public address system announcements) and
- scheduling student field trips on Fridays as much as possible.

PURPOSE OF THE STUDY

An initial external evaluation of the program, conducted in 1996-1997, indicated there was broad support for the School Division's initiative; however, questions still remained about its possible impacts. The School Division called on the Department of Education to permanently approve the initiative, but before considering the request, the Department required solid evidence that the alternative school calendar did not adversely affect student achievement. Saskatchewan Education, therefore, commissioned an extensive evaluation study that would be conducted over a two-year period (1998 to 2000). The general purpose of this evaluation was to investigate the possible educational and other impacts of alternative time allocation in the Scenic Valley School Division, so that the Department of Education would have sufficient information on which to make a decision about whether or not to permanently approve the Program for Protected Classroom Instruction.

RESEARCH QUESTIONS

The program evaluation was designed around the following research questions:

- ✔ What conclusions can be drawn from the existing literature on time allocation/time use (i.e., four-day instructional week) and student learning?

- ✔ How does the Scenic Valley School Division's time allocation/ actual time use compare with two other similar school divisions in the province?

- ✔ What are the levels of satisfaction of educators, students and parents with the four-day instructional school week initiative?

- ✔ What are the impacts of the initiative on the school community (i.e., schools, students and families)?

- ✔ What relationship is there between time allocation/actual time use (four-day instructional school week versus traditional school week) as an opportunity measure and student learning (achievement) as an outcome measure?

THE STUDY TEAM

Saskatchewan Education issued a Request for Proposals (RFP) to conduct the evaluation study; the Education Quality and Accountability Office (EQAO) was the successful bidder.[4] Two of the agency's assessment and evaluation specialists, with extensive program evaluation experience, planned and carried out the study.

EVALUATION METHODOLOGY

Preliminary Consultations

Preliminary telephone and face-to-face meetings were held with Department of Education officials to ensure there was a mutual understanding of the study's purpose, research questions, methods of data and information gathering, timeframe, deliverables, reporting requirements and audiences. In advance of the study's launch, the Department's principal contact person for the evaluation secured the cooperation of school division personnel, school administrators, staff and parents in the communities involved in the study. Prior to any data collection in the field, the study team visited the respective communities to personally introduce the project, describe the data-collection process, explain how the information would be used and reported and provide assurances that any individual information collected would remain confidential.

---

[4] EQAO is an arms-length, independent agency of the Ontario Government, established by the Legislative Assembly of Ontario through the *Education Quality and Accountability Office Act* (1996) in response to recommendations from the 1994 *Royal Commission on Learning.* The agency is responsible for the development, administration, scoring and reporting of Ontario's large-scale assessment program and coordinates the province's involvement in national and international assessments. More information about EQAO is available on the agency's Web site at www.eqao.com.

Reference Groups

All schools in the Scenic Valley School Division participated in the study. In addition, two other school divisions with socio-economic and demographic characteristics similar to Scenic Valley's were purposefully selected by Saskatchewan Education to serve as reference groups.

Reference Group 1 was a school division situated in a mainly agricultural area east of Regina (refer to Figure 7). The School Division served an area with a total population of about 12,000, almost 15 percent of whom were First Nations people. At the time of the study, the Division had a total student enrollment of 959 and a total of 64 full-time equivalent teachers (73 individuals). The school year was comprised of 197 days, with five hours of classroom instruction each day in a five-day school week. Reference Group 1 had a history of administering commercial, standardized tests at the elementary-school level, but there was no Division-wide policy on standardized testing in secondary schools. Five of the six schools in the Division participated in the program evaluation. The sixth school was scheduled to close prior to completion of the two-year evaluation and was therefore not included in the study.

Reference Group 2 was a school division located in a predominantly agricultural area northwest of Saskatoon (refer to Figure 7). The total population served by the Division was nearly 19,000, of whom about nine percent were First Nations people. At the time of the study, the Division had an enrollment of 2,554 students and employed 179 teachers (140 full-time and 39 part-time) in 16 schools. Like Reference Group 1, the Division's school year consisted of 197 days with five hours of classroom instruction per day in a five-day school week. The School Division had some experience in the use of commercial, standardized tests. Although there was no Division-wide policy regarding the administration of such tests, the use of instruments such as the Canadian Achievement Test (CAT) and the Canadian Test of Basic Skills (CTBS) was left to the discretion of individual schools and were administered to students for diagnostic purposes. The School Division's Director of Education, in consultation with Saskatchewan Education officials and the program evaluators, identified six of the Division's 16 schools for inclusion in the Scenic Valley program evaluation. This sub-set of schools was chosen to closely approximate the demographic characteristics of the other two school divisions included in the study and to ensure that about the same numbers of students in certain target grade levels would participate.

Figure 7 | Saskatchewan: Reference Groups

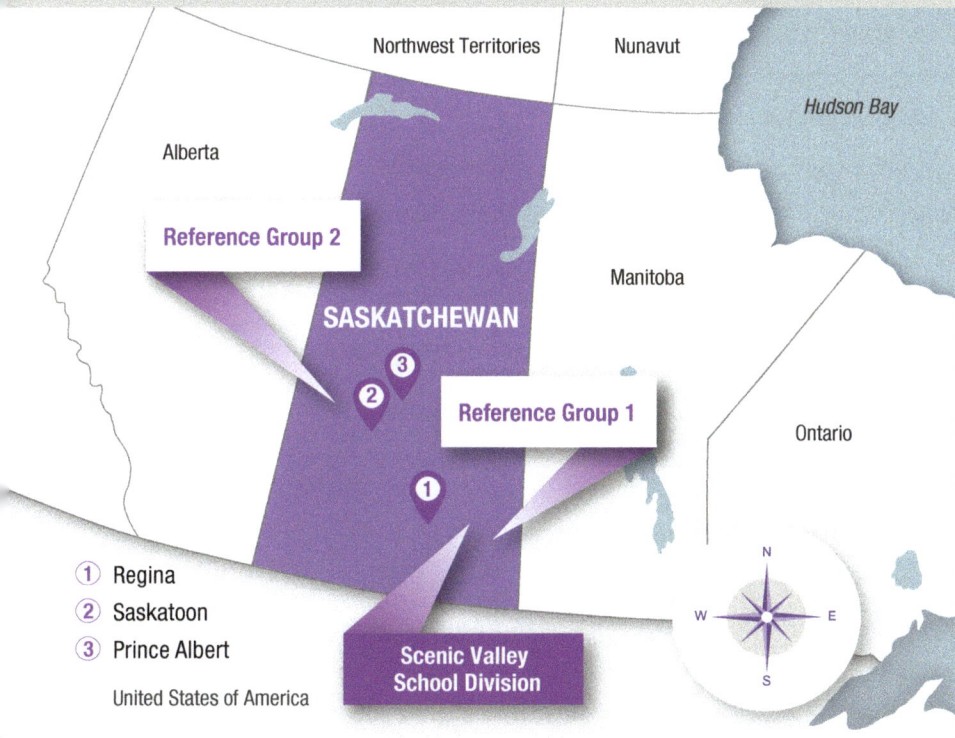

Northwest Territories

Nunavut

Hudson Bay

Alberta

Reference Group 2

SASKATCHEWAN

Manitoba

③

②

Reference Group 1

Ontario

①

N

W E

S

① Regina

② Saskatoon

③ Prince Albert

United States of America

Scenic Valley
School Division

Data-Gathering Methods

The sources of data and information to answer the study's research questions included document analysis, literature review, student achievement testing and questionnaires.

Document Analysis

Document analysis, which involved the study team's examination of school-based records such as policy documents/statements, instructional plans, timetables, bulletins and newsletters, occurred during on-site visits to the three school divisions.

Literature Review

The literature review was conducted over a four-month period. At the time of the evaluation, all significant studies concerning the four-day instructional school week were American-based and applied to rural areas where school districts had student populations of fewer than 500, dispersed over a wide geographic area. The few Canadian reports available were mainly of initial, experimental projects that had not progressed beyond the planning and pilot stages. The U.S.-based reports provided some useful information to the Scenic Valley evaluation study, but many of them noted the need for more in-depth examination of the impacts of the model on student achievement, as well as economic, social/school community and school/staff impacts.

Student Achievement Testing

The Saskatchewan Department of Education sought demonstrable evidence that would provide assurances that the four-day instructional week model was not negatively impacting student achievement. Thus, a critical component of the program evaluation centred on data gathered on student achievement in the Scenic Valley School Division and in the two Reference Groups. The evaluation study utilized the second edition of the Canadian Achievement Test (CAT/2) and the 1996 Saskatchewan Provincial Learning Assessment Program (PLAP) writing tasks to generate student achievement data. CAT/2 was a widely used standardized test that was normed in Canada. The instrument was available for students in Grades 2 to 12 and provided reliable estimates of student achievement in the areas of reading (word analysis, vocabulary and comprehension) spelling, language (language mechanics and language expression), mathematics (concepts and computation) and study skills (except for Grade 3). The PLAP writing component was included as a performance-based indicator of achievement that had the added advantage of having been specifically developed for Saskatchewan curriculum.

Student achievement testing was administered in two sessions. In the three school divisions' participating schools, all students in Grades 3, 5, 8 and 11 were involved in the first testing session in the spring of 1999, and all students in Grades 4, 6, 9 and 12 were involved in the second testing session in the spring of 2000.

A pre-test/post-test control group design was used to gather information about score changes in student achievement. Students in the three school divisions completed both test components (CAT/2 standardized tests and PLAP performance-based writing tasks) during the two testing sessions. Score gains/losses over the school year were calculated for comparison purposes. For adjacent grade levels, two different forms of the CAT/2 were used: one for the spring, 1999 and another for the spring, 2000 administrations. (The same students were involved in both testing sessions.) For example, students in Grade 3 were administered the age-/grade-appropriate CAT/2 level 13 instruments in the spring of 1999, and they were subsequently required to complete the level 14 instruments in the spring of 2000, when they were in Grade 4. The various instruments of CAT/2 had been equated, so that achievement gains/losses could be accurately measured even though different age-/grade-appropriate test instruments were used. Administration of the CAT/2 required a total of about three to three and one-half hours of class time (broken down into smaller time blocks) in each of the two testing sessions. A total of 926 students were involved in the first testing session in 1999 (Scenic Valley, 325; Reference Group 1, 302; Reference Group 2, 299), and 880 students wrote the second set of tests in 2000 (Scenic Valley, 319; Reference Group 1, 293; Reference Group 2, 268). The lower number of students in testing session two was explained by student absence, illness and relocation.

For the first testing session, students in Grades 5, 8 and 11 wrote the 1996 PLAP writing assessment, because it had been designed for those grade levels. Accordingly, the second testing session involved the same students the following year in Grades 6, 9 and 12. The themes of the writing tasks were changed for the second testing session, but the tasks, procedures and scoring schemes were parallel to those used in the first session to ensure that comparisons of achievement over time could be made. Just as with the CAT/2, a pretest/post-test control group design was used with the Saskatchewan PLAP writing assessment instruments. The PLAP writing assessment was not an on-demand writing piece; instead, it involved the students using a writing process to produce one final writing product. For this component of the assessment, two or three blocks of class time were required for each testing session.

For all testing sessions, the program evaluators distributed the testing materials to the three school division central offices for subsequent delivery to their respective schools. During the testing period, the two principal researchers visited numerous participating schools to monitor the administration of the tests and meet the school administrators and teachers to answer any questions they had about the study. Following test administration, the school divisions collected all testing material and forwarded these to the program evaluators for processing.

The CAT/2 booklets from both testing sessions (Grade 3) and machine-readable forms (Grades 5, 6, 8, 9, 11 and 12) were scanned and the data analyzed and graphed. All PLAP writing products from both testing sessions were securely stored at EQAO. Following a randomizing process, they were eventually scored by selected, volunteer teachers from the three participating school divisions during a single scoring session, which was held in Regina, in July, 2000. Using the same teachers to score all writing products helped to ensure scoring accuracy and consistency across the two testing periods. The scoring session was supervised by the EQAO researchers; the scorers were trained by a local educator with extensive prior experience in scoring and training teachers to score the PLAP writing assessments. For the purposes of this study, the writing prompts, scoring rubrics and exemplars from the 1996 PLAP in writing were used as the standards to judge writing quality. The same 1996 writing prompts were used at the Grade 8 and 12 levels; identical writing prompts were also used at the Grade 9 and 11 levels. The 1996 prompt was used for Grade 5; however, a new, but substantially similar prompt was developed for Grade 6. Because the prompts at Grades 5, 8 and 11 were the 1996 prompts, the provincially determined exemplars were used together with the 1996 training papers. For the other three grade levels (6, 9, 12), new exemplars had to be selected and matched to the existing provincial exemplars, with reference to the same criteria or rubrics. The same head scorer who had selected the 1996 provincial exemplars selected the new exemplars and matched them to the existing ones, using the same process that had been used in 1996.

At the July, 2000 scoring session, an exemplar from Grade 5 was matched with one from Grade 6 at each quality level (score code). Therefore, the scorers used two exemplars at each of the performance codes (1 to 5) in judging the work from each pair of grades. The writing products from each of the two adjacent grades were randomly mixed, so that scorers worked through bundles of ten papers including (for example) student writing products from both Grade 5 and 6. This procedure ensured that the work from the adjacent grade levels was always scored to the same standard. Six scorers with experience in teaching at least two of the grade levels were trained to score all of the student work. As part of the training process they examined the scoring rubrics and exemplars and then discussed the training papers as a whole group until they had internalized the standards by which they were to score. Then, pairs of scorers scored 20 papers first independently, then together, comparing any papers that did not receive the same score from both scorers. When the scores for these papers were resolved to the satisfaction of the scorers and the group leader, training ended and live scoring began. During each day of scoring, ten papers from each scorer were randomly and blindly re-assigned to a second scorer in order to monitor inter-rater reliability. Furthermore, each day two papers from each of Grades 5 and 6, Grades 8 and 9 and Grades 11 and 12 were selected to be scored by all scorers as another measure of inter-rater reliability. There were three days of scoring, approximately one for each pair of grades, including both the training and the scoring for the given pair of grades.

Questionnaires

During the fall of 1999, four separate surveys were distributed to all members of the main stakeholder groups in the Scenic Valley School Division: teachers, parents and students (one survey for children in Grades 1 to 3 and another for students in Grades 4 to 12). The purpose of the surveys was to gather information from the school communities about attitudes and behaviours directly related to the four-day instructional week. The educator survey included questions about the number of years of teaching experience, teaching experience with four-day and five-day instructional week schedules and specifically, with regard to the four-day instructional week, it asked questions concerning

- amount of flexibility to allow for learning abilities/styles;
- amount of disruption to instructional time;
- amount of homework;
- student participation in learning activities;
- student satisfaction;
- student stress;
- teacher classroom preparation time;
- teacher follow-up/remedial work with students;
- teacher satisfaction/enthusiasm;
- teacher sense of accomplishment;
- teacher opportunities for professional development;
- teacher ability to try new instructional methods;
- teacher opportunities for co-planning;
- teacher stress;
- team/collegial atmosphere;
- teacher opportunities for personal and school extra-curricular activities;
- teacher opportunities to meet and work with parents and
- advantages and disadvantages of the program.

The parent questionnaire asked questions concerning

- number of their children attending the Scenic Valley School Division and their grade(s) levels;
- children's satisfaction with school;
- amount of homework assigned;
- children's preparedness for class;
- teachers' ability to provide assistance to students;
- number of field trips and other school extra-curricular activities;
- children's participation in school extra-curricular activities;
- level of satisfaction with quality of children's education, including their academic achievement;
- amount of family time;
- disruptions to family routine;
- family stress level;
- children's participation in community activities;
- children's ability to help out at home;
- time for medical, dental and other appointments;
- need for child care;
- financial costs to the family;
- overall satisfaction with the four-day instructional week and
- advantages and disadvantages of the program.

The survey of Scenic Valley students in Grades 4 to 12 asked them about

- their gender;
- their grade;
- the number of years they had attended the school;
- how much they liked school;

- how the four-day instructional week affected their learning;
- their level of energy/fatigue at school;
- how the four-day instructional week affected their involvement in school activities;
- the attitude of teachers in class;
- whether the teachers had time to help students;
- the activities in which they were involved on Fridays when not at school;
- the amount of time spent on homework of various kinds;
- the amount of time spent on average each day reading for enjoyment or general interest;
- the amount of time spent per week watching television or playing video or computer games;
- the amount of time spent per week playing sports and/or taking part in school extra-curricular or community activities;
- how their parents/guardians were involved in various school activities;
- their overall satisfaction with the four-day instructional week and
- things they liked or disliked about the four-day instructional week.

A much shorter and simpler survey was administered to Scenic Valley students in Grades 1 to 3.

In all cases, respondents were informed that their individual questionnaire responses would remain confidential, and that all individual responses would be aggregated and reported to Saskatchewan Education as summary information only.

Another questionnaire, related to student writing attitudes and behaviours, was administered during the spring, 1999 testing session.
This questionnaire was included in the study design at the request of
the Directors of Education of the three participating school divisions.
The questionnaire results were of interest to the school divisions but
were not considered a formal part of the program evaluation. Consequently, data from these questionnaires, together with interpretive
guidelines, were forwarded separately to the three school divisions
for program improvement purposes.

DATA CODING, ANALYSIS AND INTERPRETATION

The teacher, parent and student surveys contained questions to which
respondents answered using checklists and Likert-type scales. Each
survey contained two or three questions which required open/writ-
ten responses. On receipt of the completed questionnaires, the study
team used content analysis to code the answers. For the most part,
data and information were summarized by descriptive statistics such
as frequency counts, percentages and means, as well as descriptive,
qualitative summaries.

With regard to student achievement testing, student responses to the
multiple-choice CAT/2 instruments were machine-scored. Options
for reporting the CAT/2 results included grade equivalence, stanines
and percentile ranks. Grade equivalent and percentile scores describe
test performance for the imaginary "average" student. Stanines, on
the other hand, account for the individual achievement of students;
the proportion of students meeting and exceeding a predetermined,
national standard is reported. For the purposes of this study, therefore,
the program evaluators selected stanines as the most meaningful way
to report student achievement results. Stanines are standard scores

based on a scale of nine equal units that range from a high of nine to a low of one. In general, stanines of one through three are considered below average achievement, four through six are considered average and seven through nine are considered above average. For the purposes of the final report, the percentage of students achieving the national stanine four and above was calculated and reported. In other words, the results reported the extent to which students in the Scenic Valley School Division and the two reference groups performed at or above the Canadian norm. (Grade equivalent and percentile scores were also generated, but they were not provided in the final report.)

Analysis of Variance (ANOVA) and paired contrasts were used to determine whether there were any statistically significant differences in the student achievement scores of Scenic Valley School Division as compared with each of the two reference groups and with the Canadian norms. These analyses were conducted by Grade (3, 5, 8 and 11 for test session one and 4, 6, 9 and 12 for test session two), by CAT/2 sub-test (e.g., reading, spelling, language, mathematics) and by total test battery. (Total test battery refers to the overall score compiled from the sub-tests.) The analyses were also conducted by gender by grade for the total test scores in each test session. A significant statistic of .05 or smaller indicated a "real" difference between scores, rather than differences that may have occurred due to chance. Such statistically significant differences in student achievement were the focus of findings presented in the report.

For the PLAP writing assessments, the percentage of students achieving at Level 3 or above (on a five-point scale) was calculated and reported. Chi-square tests were used to test the significance of differences between the Scenic Valley School Division and the two reference groups for each of the two test sessions, as well as changes (growth/loss) between sessions.

REPORTING

This program evaluation was conducted over two school years: 1998-1999 and 1999-2000. The agreement with Saskatchewan Education called for reporting in four stages. An interim report (results of the literature review) was submitted in April, 1999; interim results from test session one were submitted in July, 1999; attitudinal survey results for the Scenic Valley School Division were submitted in February, 2000 and the final report, which contained the final version of the literature review, the results from both test sessions, all questionnaire findings, answers to the research questions and overall conclusions, was submitted to the Department in August of 2000.

SUMMARY

The program evaluation of the Scenic Valley School Division's Program for Protected Classroom instruction was conducted to provide the Saskatchewan Department of Education with data and information to make a decision about whether or not to approve the permanent implementation of the four-day instructional week model. The Evaluation for Decision Making approach generated data and information about context, inputs, processes and products associated with the Scenic Valley initiative. The evaluation study was considered to be successful in that reports were submitted in a timely fashion according to the project schedule; all of the research questions were answered and Saskatchewan Education was satisfied that the review had met its objectives and yielded sufficient quality information on which to base decisions about the future of the program.

The following aspects of the evaluation's methodology demonstrate the many ways in which *The Program Evaluation Standards, Guiding Principles for Evaluators, Principles for Fair Student Assessment*

Practices for Education in Canada and *Standards for Educational and Psychological Testing* were incorporated into the study:

- The evaluation was conducted by an experienced team which used effective program evaluation and project management strategies.

- Student achievement testing was an important data-gathering method in this evaluation. Great care was taken to select appropriate reference groups and assessment instruments/methods, ensure the assessments were properly administered and scored and make certain that results were correctly interpreted and reported.

- The study provided stakeholders (Department of Education and school divisions) with relevant, reliable information for decision-making and for making educational improvements, respectively.

- Effective communication with the Department of Education, school division personnel (including teachers), students and their parents at all stages of the evaluation ensured transparency of the study and that the needs of stakeholders were met.

- Assurances were made to all study participants that their individual data/information would be kept strictly confidential; procedures were instituted to ensure this occurred.

- All aspects of the evaluation, including agreements about the purposes, study design, procedures, data/information and results were clearly and fully documented.

- Reports related to students' writing attitudes and behaviours were provided to the three school divisions together with interpretive guidelines to prevent misinterpretation of findings.

CRITICISM AS EVALUATION (CONNOISSEURSHIP)

CRITICISM AS EVALUATION (CONNOISSEURSHIP)

The Insurance Institute of Canada Examinations Study

BACKGROUND AND CONTEXT OF THE STUDY

At the time of this study (1999), the Insurance Institute of Canada was a non-profit, educational organization in the property/casualty insurance industry with headquarters in Toronto, Ontario. Through the organization, students were able to take a series of 12 technical insurance courses and wrote national examinations leading to the profession-al designation of Associate of the Insurance Institute of Canada (AIIC). Graduates of these courses used this des-ignation on their business cards and correspondence to denote a high level of educational achievement and pro-fessionalism. The AIIC designation was widely recognized and well-regarded within the insurance industry. Beyond this level, the Fellowship program (FIIC) was a series of 10 courses offered by the major Canadian universities through their departments of continuing education. The Associate-ship program was the focus of this evaluation study.

Figure 8 | The Insurance Institute of Canada: Location of Institutes and Chapters

Location of Institutes and Chapters:

1. Vancouver, BC
2. Edmonton, AB
3. Calgary, AB
4. Regina, SK
5. Winnipeg, MB
6. Toronto, ON
7. Kitchener, ON
8. London, ON
9. Hamilton, ON
10. Ottawa, ON
11. Montréal, QC
12. St. John's, NL
13. Moncton, NB
14. Charlottetown, PE
15. Dartmouth, NS

The Insurance Institute had approximately 32,000 members across Canada. The organization enrolled about 16,000 students and processed in the order of 20,000 examination booklets annually. At the time of this study, there had been more than 10,000 graduates of the Institute. Students were able to take courses by attending evening classes or by correspondence. In total, 26 courses were offered by the Institute, and six of the 12 Associateship program courses were mandatory. Textbooks for the courses were written by industry experts in collaboration with the Institute's staff editors and were available in Canada's two official languages (French and English).

Three examination sessions were held annually in April, July and December. Provincial institutes across the country (refer to Figure 8) arranged for local examination centres and proctors to supervise test administration. For any given course, all students wrote the same test at the same time across the country. The examinations of the Associateship program were three hours in length and, in all but one course, were made up exclusively of open-response questions/tasks. Following the examinations, the test booklets were scored by industry professionals who were paid a fee for providing the service on their own time. Each scorer was given a particular question, a set of questions or a full booklet to score, and that person was responsible for scoring all of the responses to the question, set of questions or complete booklet from across the country. This procedure was meant to ensure fair, consistent and reliable scoring of student work. As was mentioned previously, the examinations were developed by retired industry practitioners who had a great deal of expertise and knowledge in the insurance industry. However, these individuals had no formal training in test preparation or student evaluation.

PURPOSE OF THE STUDY

When the examinations program was initially established, the Institute's Academic Council and the Board of Governors favoured the open-response format, which they believed was most appropriate given the courses' objectives. However, because of the test format, the need to hand-score all student responses and the data analysis time requirements, it often took three months or more before students received their results. Not only did the students want their results returned more promptly, but also within the Institute there had been some discussion about the possible use and appropriateness of other examination formats such as objective (multiple-choice) items (questions) which would allow for quicker reporting. Consequently, the Insurance Institute of Canada decided that it would commission a comprehensive evaluation of the Associateship's examinations and processes, including recommendations for program improvement.

RESEARCH QUESTIONS

The examinations study (or program review) was designed to answer the following research questions.

To what extent are the Associateship examinations appropriate with regard to

- ✔ content;
- ✔ technical quality;
- ✔ types and proportion/balance of questions;
- ✔ suitability of the questions and examinations in evaluating student learning in light of the course objectives, materials and textbooks;

- ✔ question difficulty levels and proportion/weighting of questions at varying difficulty levels;
- ✔ time/length of examinations;
- ✔ quality of training for scorers, scoring keys and guidelines and other materials for scorers and
- ✔ examination development process and reporting formats?

THE STUDY TEAM

A Request for Proposals (RFP) was issued, and the Education Quality and Accountability Office (EQAO) was contracted to conduct an independent review of the program.[5] EQAO was selected to carry out the evaluation because of the agency's responsibility for the development, administration, scoring and reporting of Ontario's provincial large-scale student assessment program; its coordination of the province's participation in national and international assessments and its reputation for excellence in large-scale assessment. Furthermore, the study team consisted of two experienced evaluation experts, one of whom had served as a senior manager of assessment programs in three Canadian provinces and had a strong reputation for conducting successful program evaluations. The evaluators, therefore, were considered to be evaluation connoisseurs: competent to examine evidence and bring theory and experience to bear in making critical judgements about the Associateship examinations program.

---

[5] EQAO is an arms-length, independent agency of the Ontario Government, established by the Legislative Assembly of Ontario through the *Education Quality and Accountability Office Act* (1996) in response to recommendations from the 1994 *Royal Commission on Learning.* The agency is responsible for the development, administration, scoring and reporting of Ontario's large-scale assessment program and coordinates the province's involvement in national and international assessments. More information about EQAO is available on the agency's Web site at www.eqao.com.

EVALUATION METHODOLOGY

The program review was conducted over a five-month period from March to July, 1999. Prior to launching the review, the evaluators met with the Institute's Registrar (who served as the key point of contact for the study) to discuss details of the evaluation methodology and come to an understanding about deliverables and timelines. It was agreed that the study team would provide the Institute with a final report in July in conjunction with a briefing of the organization's Board of Governors. Examination and document review, test and item statistics review, and telephone surveys were the information sources to address the research questions.

Examination and Document Review

Examination and document reviews were the principal methods of data and information collection. Using these methods, the evaluators were able to evaluate the structure, content and quality of the examinations, as well as the development, scoring and reporting processes and products. The study team decided (in consultation with the Institute) that a review of a sample of 10 courses (e.g., Insurance Against Crime, Automobile Insurance, Introduction to Personal Lines Insurance, Insurance on Property, Insurance Against Liability) would be sufficient for the purposes of the study, because all 26 courses and associated documents and examinations were similarly designed. The review included all relevant materials associated with the courses: instructor's handbook, textbooks, test instruments, training and scoring materials, data related to student enrolments and success rates in various instructional centres across the country and test item (question) statistical data. Other than textbooks, no other teaching materials or documents related to examination development (e.g., framework documents, test blueprints, test development guidelines) were available.

All of the examinations for the 10 courses for December, 1998 and a selection of examinations for April, 1999 were analyzed. In addition, an in-depth, longitudinal content analysis of examinations for two courses was conducted over four time periods between April, 1998 and April, 1999. Each question and part-question was described in terms of the course of study from which it was derived, and the following information was recorded:

- The subject matter of the question
- The number of pages of information referred to
- The number of pages in each study (topic) of the course
- The topic or section heading referred to
- The number of sections/topics in the course

This information was used as a measure of the extent to which the examinations represented the breadth of information in the course. In addition, examinations were carefully reviewed with reference to well-established standards of best practice for item and test development. The study team also analyzed a selection of "Answer Points" documents to determine their adequacy as scoring guides.

Attention was also given to identifying where course material could be assessed using multiple-choice as opposed to open-response items/ tasks. This was accomplished by analyzing the language (particularly the verbs) used in the studies' (topics') stated objectives. For example, if the focus of the objective was on remembering specific information and used verbs such as "identify," "recall" or "list," there was the possibility for the use of closed-response (e.g., multiple-choice) items. On the other hand, when students were expected to "describe," "compare," or "discuss" (for example), then the open-response item format was considered appropriate.

Test and Item Statistics Review

The study team retained the services of a well-known testing expert and psychometrician to collaborate on the review and analysis of overall test data and test-item statistics. Test and item statistics were analyzed to determine the difficulty of individual items and the examination overall and to identify any signs of problems with item quality and examination length.

Telephone Surveys

An important aspect of the review was to elicit information on the effectiveness and relevance of the examinations from the perspectives of the various participant groups. Consequently, the program review called for telephone surveys of three categories of people associated with the Associateship program: course authors, student graduates and examination scorers. The Insurance Institute of Canada provided the study team with lists of names for each of these groups from which random samples of two course authors, 20 student graduates (two for each of the 10 courses) and 10 scorers were selected. The telephone surveys were conducted during a two-week period in June, 1999. The surveys were semi-structured in that each respondent in each of the three categories was asked the same open-ended questions; however, the interviewer was able to probe for more detailed information. The interviewer took notes during the interviews and informed each respondent that his/her responses would be kept anonymous and confidential.

Course authors were asked for the following types of information:

- The credentials, training and experience that prepared them to be course and examination developers
- A step-by-step description of how they developed an examination

- The extent to which the examination format (open-response) matched the way in which people in the insurance industry applied the course content in their day-to-day work and whether or not other formats (e.g., multiple-choice items) would be appropriate

- Suggestions for how the Insurance Institute of Canada might change its examination development and scoring process to improve efficiency and effectiveness and provide a faster turnaround time in reporting individual student results

Student graduates were asked for the following types of information:

- Their level of satisfaction with the turnaround time between writing an examination and receiving their results

- Fairness of the Insurance Institute's examinations in terms of course alignment, level of difficulty and how they were scored

- The extent to which the examination format (open-response) matched the way in which people in the insurance industry applied the course content in their day-to-day work and whether or not other formats (e.g., multiple-choice items) would be appropriate

- Suggestions for improving the Insurance Institute's examination process with respect to examination format, length and information/feedback received in individual student reports

Examination scorers were asked for the following types of information:

- How well prepared they believed they were for their scoring responsibilities (including background/reference materials, training materials, scoring guidelines, answer keys)

- Length of time to score a question, block of questions or full examination

- Ways in which the scoring process could be streamlined or altered to achieve a faster turnaround time in reporting individual student results

- The extent to which the examination format (open-response) matched the way in which people in the insurance industry applied the course content in their day-to-day work and whether or not other formats (e.g., multiple-choice items) would be appropriate

- Fairness of the Insurance Institute's examinations with respect to their level of difficulty

- Suggestions about how the Insurance Institute might improve the efficiency, reliability and fairness of the scoring process

DATA CODING, ANALYSIS AND INTERPRETATION

Each examination was described in terms of the number of questions (and part-questions) and the number of marks assigned to each, the number of students that sat the examination, the average score on the test, the number of examination topics in the text and the number of topics that were reflected in the test questions. Tables and item statistics were also generated for each question with descriptive statistics including the associated topic number, objective(s), number of pages referenced, number of pages on the topic, cognitive task demand, level of difficulty, mark value and success rate. Following each table, interpretive comments, summarizing the key observations (including item/question quality), were provided. The notes from all telephone surveys were reviewed by the study team; content analysis was used to code the information and the results were summarized for each respondent group.

The findings from the analyses of test documents, statistics and telephone surveys were considered in addressing each of the study's research questions.

REPORTING

The final report of the program review was submitted on schedule to the Insurance Institute of Canada in conjunction with a briefing of the Institute's Board of Governors. The report fully documented all aspects of the study and included

- an Executive Summary;
- the background to the study (including the context, purposes and research questions);
- the detailed research methodology;
- findings related to the examinations' structure; suitability of question types and content; format, layout, style and presentation; proportion of item difficulty levels; quality/clarity of questions; quantity of questions and time to complete the tests;
- findings related to examination scoring;
- overall test and item-level statistical tables;
- interview questions and anonymous individual survey responses and
- specific conclusions and recommendations.

SUMMARY

The Insurance Institute of Canada commissioned EQAO (and the specific study team) to conduct the review of the Associateship examinations program, because the evaluators were viewed as connoisseurs (possessing the knowledge and experience of large-scale, standardized assessment and program evaluation) capable of making critical judgements about various aspects of the program. A measure of the strength of the review and of the client's satisfaction with the outcome of the study was the fact that some years later, the principal evaluator was asked to conduct a follow-up program evaluation for the Institute.

The following illustrates the many ways in which this program evaluation integrated *The Program Evaluation Standards* and *Guiding Principles for Evaluators* in this study:

- Experienced program evaluators with expertise in large-scale, standardized student achievement testing comprised the study team.

- The evaluators enlisted technical support when required. Because neither member of the team had comprehensive statistical expertise, a well-respected psychometrician with achievement testing experience was hired to conduct the reviews of test and item statistics.

- Good communication was critical to this study. The evaluation was conducted in a very short timeframe, so it was imperative that the client and the evaluators had a clear understanding of the purposes of the study and its specific research questions, the methodology that would be used, the data/information that would be generated and the types of recommendations that would be possible. There was no time for misunderstandings, and there could be no surprises.

- The evaluation employed a sound design which addressed the purposes and specific research questions.

- Although the study primarily involved reviews of documents, examinations and statistics, telephone interviews with individuals involved in various ways with the program provided valuable insights. Care was taken to ensure interviewees that their personal information and individual responses would remain anonymous and confidential.

- The study met the intended purposes. The client was satisfied that the review yielded quality, reliable data and information, as well as sound recommendations for making decisions about the format of the Associateship examinations and for effecting improvements to the examinations program.

ONTARIO

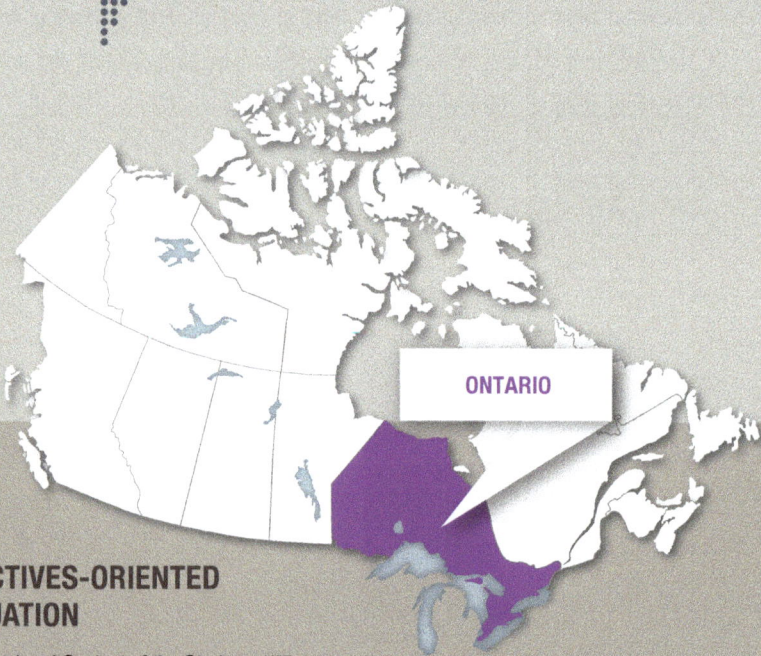

OBJECTIVES-ORIENTED
EVALUATION

OBJECTIVES-ORIENTED EVALUATION

12

Ontario Academic Course Teacher In-service Program

BACKGROUND AND CONTEXT OF THE STUDY

Assessment and Accountability in Ontario

In the decades prior to the mid-1960s, the province of Ontario had a history of administering large-scale assessments, including departmental high-school exit examinations, which were used primarily as a screening device for university entrance. During the following two decades, standardized student achievement testing was abandoned.

Earl (1995) stated that

> **In the 1970s and early 1980s, when many other provinces and American states were expanding their assessment programs, Ontario left assessment in the hands of educators at the district level. Teachers were expected to develop evaluation procedures and examinations that measured the achievement of students in specified courses and programs based on provincial curriculum guidelines, as outlined in a provincial policy document covering Grades 7 through 12.** (p. 46)

During the 1980s, concerns began to surface about the perceived inequality of standards in the province's secondary schools; there were questions about whether students had acquired the necessary knowledge and skills required for the world of work or post-secondary education; there was growing evidence that the public was losing confidence in the education system and universities began to call for a return to province-wide examinations.

As the pressure for greater accountability grew, the Ministry of Education initiated several programs in the mid-1980s. For example, in 1986, the Ministry implemented a series of nine program reviews in Grade 9 geography, senior chemistry and physics, Grade 6 reading and mathematics, Grade 8 mathematics, Grade 10 mathematics and Grade 12 mathematics and writing. These reviews involved student achievement testing in random samples of schools and were meant to evaluate the effectiveness of the various programs, as well as provide information for program improvement (Earl, 1995).

Ontario Academic Course Teacher In-service Program

Also in the mid-1980s, the ministry began a program of examination reviews and teacher in-service focused on the OAC level (the final year of secondary education). The Ontario Academic Course Teacher In-service Program (OAC-TIP) was implemented, at least in part, because of the perception that there was considerable variability in how student marks were awarded province-wide, and so the examination reviews focused on the adequacy of teacher-developed examinations and how they were marked. The program was implemented as a quality-control or moderating process to ensure greater consistency in how students' marks in OAC courses were derived and awarded across the province and to provide OAC teachers with professional development to improve their classroom assessment practices. The specific purposes of OAC-TIP were as follows:

- To ensure implementation of the Ministry's criteria for assessing student achievement at the OAC level
- To increase consistency in the development and marking of OAC examinations
- To refine final marks policy
- To provide professional development for teachers

All publicly funded and inspected private schools offering OAC courses were expected to participate in OAC-TIP. The entire review process took approximately four to five years to complete and consisted of five sequential stages: research, development, implementation, review and maintenance/follow-up.

During the research stage, a study was conducted in a representative sample of Ontario secondary schools and involved examining the OAC assessment practices in the given subject under review. This process included gathering data via teacher questionnaires, collecting and analyzing OAC examinations and conducting on-site interviews with teachers.

In the **development** stage, a draft teacher handbook was written based on best practices as identified through the research study. The handbook reflected provincial expectations as articulated in the specific OAC curriculum guideline of the subject under review.

In the **implementation** stage, one-day workshops to implement the handbook were provided to teachers in the given OAC subject in various locations throughout the province.

In the **review** stage, each secondary school offering the given OAC subject was required to submit one set of assessment materials, including examinations and associated marking schemes; three marked student responses representing high, medium and low achievement and a completed teacher questionnaire. The Ministry of Education assembled a review team in Toronto to analyze the sets of assessment-related material to determine the extent to which they were consistent with provincial expectations as reflected in the draft handbook and the provincial curriculum guideline. Following the review, school, school board and provincial reports were prepared and distributed by the Ministry. Schools that did not conform satisfactorily to the Ministry guidelines were expected to re-submit their assessment materials the next time the course was offered.

During the **maintenance/follow-up** stage, the handbook for the given subject was further refined (based on information obtained through the review process) and was distributed to all publicly funded and inspected private secondary schools offering OAC courses.

During the approximately 10-year life of the program, examination reviews were conducted in English Language and Literature,

Français, English/Anglais, French as a Second Language, Core and Extended/Immersion, Visual Arts, Calculus, Accounting, Economics, Chemistry, Physics, Geography, History and Contemporary Studies and Family Studies (Jones, 1998).

PURPOSE OF THE STUDY

In the original design of OAC-TIP, there was no provision made for a formal review or evaluation of the program itself. Although there was strong support for the program on the part of educators, there was no available data/information on the extent to which the program was meetings its objectives. In addition, with the Ministry of Education's 1995 announcement about secondary school reform, it was evident that the program would have to change to be consistent with new directions in the provincial education system. The primary purpose of the program evaluation, therefore, was to provide the Ministry with information about the extent to which the various objectives of OAC-TIP had been met. A secondary purpose was to suggest how the program could be improved or changed.

RESEARCH QUESTIONS

The program evaluation was designed around the following issues and research questions:

Issue: Objectives of the Program

✔ To what extent have the Ministry's criteria for assessing student achievement at the OAC level been implemented?

✔ To what extent is there consistency in how OAC examinations are designed and marked?

✔ To what extent has OAC-TIP contributed to refining final marks policy?

✔ To what extent does OAC-TIP provide professional development for teachers?

✔ To what extent do the program's objectives remain valid?

✔ Are there additional issues or areas of concern the program should address?

Issue: Program Design and Implementation

✔ Are there ways the program can be improved?

✔ What recommendations can be made toward the design and implementation of a new quality-control program?

THE STUDY TEAM

The evaluation was conducted by a two-person team of experienced evaluators who represented the English and French sections of the Education Quality and Accountability Office (EQAO).[6] Two groups supported the work of the study team. EQAO's Assessment Advisory Committee, representing all of the agency's major stakeholder groups, provided consultation on the project's proposal, the study's findings and draft reports. A steering committee of individuals with a broad range of experience with the OAC-TIP processes advised the study team on the design of the data-collection instruments and the content and format of reports.

---

[6] EQAO is an arms-length, independent agency of the Ontario Government, established by the Legislative Assembly of Ontario through the *Education Quality and Accountability Office Act* (1996) in response to recommendations from the 1994 *Royal Commission on Learning*. The agency is responsible for the development, administration, scoring and reporting of Ontario's large-scale assessment program and coordinates the province's involvement in national and international assessments. More information about EQAO is available on the agency's Web site at www.eqao.com.

EVALUATION METHODOLOGY

The evaluation of OAC-TIP, from initial design to reporting, took place over a ten-month period from February to November, 1996. The study team used questionnaires, focus-group consultations and Ministry of Education documents and records to gather the data and information required to answer the research questions.

Questionnaires

A stratified random sample of 100 English-language and 50 French-language publicly funded and inspected private secondary schools (representing all regions of the province) was drawn, and all teachers in the schools who had participated in an OAC-TIP review were expected to complete a questionnaire (refer to Figure 9). In addition, school principals and vice-principals of the selected schools, as well as school board superintendents and consultants of the school boards associated with the selected schools were also expected to complete the questionnaire. Respondents were asked not to identify themselves on the questionnaire to ensure anonymity. In total, 683 questionnaires (509 English-language and 174 French-language) were completed and returned to the study team. Although there was no personal identifying information on the questionnaires, many of the return envelopes had school addresses affixed to them. An examination of the school addresses indicated that the completed questionnaires represented a good cross-section of the province.

Focus-Group Consultations

Semi-structured, focus-group consultations were conducted in separate English and French meetings. In each language, consultation meetings were conducted with four types of groups as follows:

1. OAC-level teachers from a provincially representative cross-section of 30 English- and 15 French-language schools

2. Education partner organizations such as the Ontario Teachers' Federation (and affiliates), colleges and universities, parent groups and subject associations

3. Representatives of the Ministry of Education curriculum, policy and curriculum reform units, as well as EQAO education officers, most of whom had some involvement with OAC-TIP

4. Staff of the Ministry and EQAO who had been directly involved in OAC-TIP activities such as distribution, receipt and tracking of materials, data entry and database management and report development

The first type of focus group involved a total of 30 English and 15 French OAC-level teachers, one from each school sampled; the second type of focus group involved approximately 25 representatives from the various organizations and the third and fourth types of focus groups involved a combined total of approximately 20 staff members.

Ministry of Education Documents and Records

Ministry of Education documents and records, including OAC-TIP provincial, school board and school reports and associated databases, were also analyzed for data and information relevant to the program evaluation.

Figure 9 | Ontario: Education Regions and Regional Offices

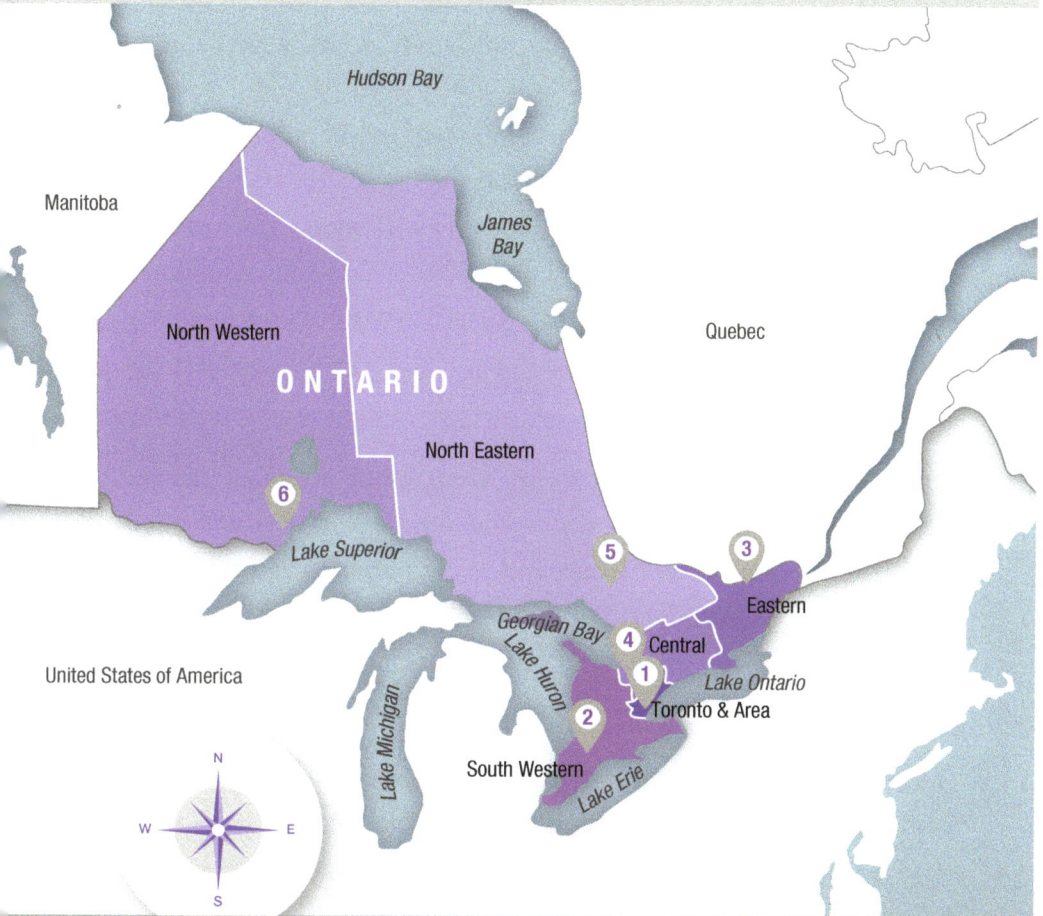

Figure 9 | Ontario: Education Regions and Regional Offices

Ministry of Education Regional Offices:

1. Toronto and Area Regional Office
2. London Regional Office
3. Ottawa Regional Office
4. Barrie Regional Office
5. North Bay/Sudbury Regional Office
6. Thunder Bay Regional Office

Education Regions:

- North Western
- North Eastern
- Central
- Eastern
- Toronto & Area
- South Western

DATA CODING, ANALYSIS AND INTERPRETATION

A series of descriptive statistics was generated and organized by sub-ject review. For the most part, percentages, (e.g., the percentage of schools that participated in each subject review; the percentage of schools that conformed to various components of the Ministry guide-lines; the percentage of educators who indicated they had attended a provincial workshop as part of the OAC-TIP review; the percent-age of educators who indicated the OAC-TIP handbooks, guidelines, workshops and reports were useful; the percentage of educators that indicated they continued to follow the guidelines) were used to pres-ent the evaluation findings.

The findings from the questionnaires, focus-group consultations and Ministry documents and records provided sufficient data and infor-mation to respond to the two general study purposes and to answer the evaluation's research questions.

REPORTING

The final report of the OAC-TIP program review was submitted to the Ministry of Education on schedule in November, 1996. The re-port fully documented the evaluation study and contained the follow-ing elements:

- Background and context of the study
- OAC-TIP program description
- Purpose of the program review
- Research issues and questions
- Detailed methodology
- Review findings by research issue and question, including sta-tistical tables and associated graphs
- Study conclusions and recommendations

SUMMARY

The general purposes of the Ontario Academic Course Teacher In-service Program (OAC-TIP) study were to provide the Ministry of Education with information about the extent to which the program was successful in meeting its various objectives and to identify areas for program improvement. Because EQAO was an independent Crown agency in the province of Ontario, most stakeholders outside of government would have viewed the study as an external evaluation; however, many Ministry and EQAO personnel perceived this as an internal program evaluation.

Several elements contributed to a successful evaluation:

- The study team comprised two experienced evaluators who had been associated with OAC-TIP and represented both of Canada's official languages (English and French).

- OAC-TIP was a provincial secondary-school program; consequently, many individuals and organizations had an interest in the program and its review. The study team used this to advantage by incorporating ongoing communication with the principal stakeholder groups into the evaluation design and by directly involving stakeholders in the evaluation process.

- Apart from the analysis of Ministry documents and records, the study relied primarily on information derived from questionnaires and focus groups. The interactions with all participants were conducted in a respectful manner, and all information from individuals was kept strictly confidential.

- The evaluation design was successful in generating the data and information required by the Ministry of Education to make decisions about the future of the program.

ONTARIO

APPRAISAL

APPRAISAL
Ensuring Quality
Assessments Review

13

BACKGROUND AND CONTEXT OF THE STUDY

History of Assessment in Ontario

In the decades prior to the mid-1960s, Ontario had a tradition of standardized student assessment. During the 1950s and 1960s, for instance, students in Grade 13 were required to write departmental examinations (high-school exit exams) in all subject areas that served as the sole basis for university entrance. This changed in the mid-1960s, as teacher marks were combined with examination marks in the given subjects to derive final student results.

After 1967, the departmental examinations were discontinued, and teacher-awarded marks became the sole basis for university entrance. In the 1970s and early 1980s, while other Canadian provinces and U.S. states were expanding their assessment programs, Ontario left student assessment in the hands of educators. Teachers were given a great deal of autonomy in developing their own assessments and in making judgements about the quality of students' work (Royal Commission on Learning, 1994).

During the 1980s, the province undertook a series of provincial reviews (described in Chapter 12), and in the mid-1980s and early 1990s, it began to participate in national and international assessments. For example, Ontario took part in the Council of Ministers of Education, Canada's (CMEC) School Achievement Indicators Program (SAIP), a national assessment program which was initiated in 1993 and tested 13- and 16-year-old students in mathematics, reading and writing and science. (The SAIP has since been replaced by the Pan-Canadian Assessment Program [PCAP] that assesses Grade 8 students.) In 1995, the province also participated in the Third International Mathematics and Science Study (TIMSS), which involved students in Grades 3, 4, 7, 8, as well as secondary school. These national and international studies used random samples of schools and students. This approach, although economical, did not allow for reporting of results at the individual student, school or school board levels; only provincial outcomes were available. In general, the results of these studies indicated that the performance of Ontario students was essentially in the "middle of the pack" (adequate but not outstanding) when compared to the outcomes of other participating provinces and countries. The results of these studies contributed to the public discussion and concern about the quality of the Ontario education system.

During the 1980s an early 1990s, there was growing evidence that the public was losing confidence in the education system, and pressure was mounting to report on the quality of education in Ontario schools. School systems were under pressure to provide their publics with information about what schools were doing and the extent to which their efforts were achieving results. Furthermore, educators and policy makers were realizing that they needed better information to make good decisions, monitor reform efforts and identify areas for corrective action/improvement (Earl, 1995).

The Education Quality and Accountability Office

In May 1993, the Province of Ontario established the Royal Commission on Learning to ensure that Ontario's youth would be well-prepared for the challenges of the twenty-first century. After a comprehensive public consultation process, the Commission released its report, entitled *For the Love of Learning,* which suggested a vision and action plan to guide the reform of elementary and secondary education, including systems of accountability and educational governance. In response to the recommendations from the 1994 report of the Royal Commission on Learning, the Legislative Assembly of Ontario established EQAO as a Crown agency through *The Education Quality and Accountability Office Act* of 1996.[7]

The agency reports on the quality and effectiveness of the province's elementary and secondary school system and the public accountability of school boards primarily through the reporting of data and infor-

---

[7] EQAO is an agency of the Ontario government, led by a Chief Executive Officer and governed by a board of directors. Its mandate is to support and guide student improvement by providing credible information about the quality of the province's publicly funded elementary and secondary education system. It does this by developing, administering, scoring and reporting on province-wide tests of elementary and secondary school students' achievement in reading, writing and mathematics in relation to *Ontario Curriculum* learning expectations. The agency also manages and reports on the province's participation in national and international testing programs.

mation derived in conjunction with a provincial student assessment program. Some key principles of the assessments are that

- they are directly linked to the learning expectations of *The Ontario Curriculum;*
- all students are expected to participate (they are census rather than sample assessments);
- they are performance-based, in that open-response as well as closed-response items/tasks are included, so that students have a variety of ways to demonstrate their knowledge and abilities;
- educators are involved in all aspects of test development, administration and scoring and
- the assessments are developed separately but in parallel and in equal quality in both of Canada's official languages (English and French).

The first EQAO large-scale assessment was the 1996-1997 Grade 3 reading, writing and mathematics assessment in which all students participated. According to Wolfe, Childs and Elgie (2004), the assessment involved performance tests that had students writing, reading, writing about reading and doing mathematics activities. The test was embedded in regular classroom settings as part of instructional units that required about 12 hours of testing over a two-week period. The tests were developed as authentic representations of classroom activity, and evaluation was conducted by teams of trained teachers using holistic scoring. According to the authors,

> **This was one of the largest comprehensive assessment programs anywhere in the world, considering the depth, seriousness, and sheer magnitude of student performance testing.** (p. i)

In the years that followed, EQAO added more assessments to the annual assessment program, including a Grade 6 assessment of reading, writing and mathematics that was introduced in 1998-1999 and required the same amount of class time as the Grade 3 assessment; a Grade 9 assessment of mathematics that was introduced in 2000-2001 and an Ontario Secondary School Literacy Test (OSSLT) — a Grade 10 reading and writing test — that was initiated in 2002 and was a graduation requirement. Each of the secondary school assessments required about five hours of testing over two days.

PURPOSE OF THE STUDY

EQAO's first assessments were expansive and attempted to serve a variety of purposes. According to Wolfe, et al. (2004), EQAO's assessment program

> ...is one of the most extensive systems of performance-based educational evaluation in the world. Extraordinary efforts have been made to connect the tests to the curriculum contents, to maintain authentic links to classroom practices, and to attend to the multiplicity of purposes of assessment, including individual reporting, modelling evaluation practice, encouraging capacity building around the curriculum and evaluation, and providing information for school improvement and school and board accountability. (p. 1)

In addition, during the first years of the assessment program, changes were occurring in the provincial education system. For example, new curriculum documents were introduced by the Ministry of Education together with new report cards; in 2003-2004, the Ministry created a new course: the Ontario Secondary School Literacy Course (another avenue for some students to obtain the secondary school literacy credit for graduation) and there were calls from some educators for shorter EQAO assessments, as they believed the assessments were intrusive in schools and occupied too much classroom time.

One mark of a successful organization is that it periodically reviews the effectiveness of its practices. In November 2002, five years after the first tests were administered, EQAO's Board of Directors launched the Ensuring Quality Assessments review. The purpose of the initiative was

> **...to conduct a comprehensive review of all aspects of the EQAO assessment program to ensure that current international standards are met, that exemplary practices in large-scale assessment are matched, and that EQAO reporting practices meet user needs for accountability, improvement planning and staff development.** (Education Quality and Accountability Office, 2004, p. 3)

RESEARCH TOPICS AND QUESTIONS

A series of broad topics for deep exploration, as well as specific research questions, drove the assessment review. In considering the characteristics of an excellent assessment program, the 1993 document *Principles for Fair Student Assessment Practices for Education in Canada* was an important reference.

The *Principles* document includes a section which outlines the following six principles for mandated assessment programs:

" Developers and Users should:

1 | Inform all persons with a stake in the assessment (administrators, teachers, students, parents/guardians) of the purpose(s) of the assessment, the uses to be made of the results, and who has access to them.

2 | Design and describe procedures for developing or choosing the methods of assessment, selecting students where sampling is used, administering the assessment materials, and scoring and summarizing student responses.

3 | Interpret results in light of factors that might influence them. Important factors to consider include characteristics of the students, opportunity to learn, and comprehensiveness and representativeness of the assessment method in terms of the learning outcomes to be reported on.

4 | Specify procedures for reporting, storing, controlling access to, and destroying results.

5 | Ensure reports and explanations of results are consistent with the purpose(s) of the assessment, the intended uses of the results and the planned access to the results.

6 | Provide reports and explanations of results that can be readily understood by the intended audience(s). If necessary, employ multiple reports designed for different audiences. (p. 20) "

In consideration of the aforementioned principles, the following six broad topics, reflecting the stages of development of an assessment program, were given thorough examination:

- Clarifying assessment purposes
- Defining constructs
- Designing tests
- Developing test items and tests
- Scoring student responses
- Reporting results

In addition to the preceding topics, the following research questions formed the basis for further research on reporting, as well as capacity building:

- ✔ What should EQAO report on?
- ✔ What should the EQAO report(s) look like?
- ✔ How important is the professional development/teacher training aspect of EQAO's work?

THE STUDY TEAM

The Ensuring Quality Assessments review included elements of both internal and external evaluation. The internal evaluation components involved several EQAO researchers, education and assessment officers and members of the senior management team who conducted studies of other jurisdictions, facilitated a consultation process and analyzed and synthesized evaluation information. The external review of EQAO's assessment processes was conducted by a team of assessment and measurement experts from the Ontario Institute for Studies in Education of the University of Toronto (OISE/UT), who consulted with internationally recognized technical advisors from across Canada and the United States. EQAO commissioned the OISE/UT team to conduct this work following a Request for Quotations (RFQ) competitive process.

EVALUATION METHODOLOGY

Data-Gathering Methods

The review, which took place over an approximately one-year period, used research and study and consultation as the main data- and information-collection methods.

Research and Study

EQAO provided the OISE/UT team with access to its assessment materials, assessment data, supporting documents and staff. In addition, the office arranged for discussions with educators who had participated in the scoring sessions. Over a ten-month period, the external team systematically examined all aspects of EQAO's assessments, and in the process, numerous consultation papers were developed by the expert advisors. The final external report provided comprehensive information about

- clarifying the purposes and test designs;
- defining the constructs and specifying the curriculum connections;
- designing the assessment programs, including possible design options;
- item and test development, item banking and documentation systems;

- scoring and scaling student responses, equating between administrations and alignment to standards;

- levels of reporting, score reliability, score validity, item mapping, incomplete student work and timing of results and

- a future quality agenda, including validity research, ongoing technical advice and long-term planning and reviews.

During this same time period, EQAO researchers conducted an extensive review of best practices used by noteworthy testing organizations and jurisdictions worldwide. This review, which was conducted through the use of Internet searches and telephone interviews, focused on the same six broad assessment topics previously identified. The outcome of this research was a detailed compilation of findings organized by the six assessment topics.

Consultation

Also during the same 10-month period, EQAO held dialogue forums with the agency's Assessment Advisory Committee (including members of all of the major education stakeholder organizations) and representatives from more than 20 groups, such as directors of education, supervisory officers, principals, teachers, school board contacts, school board trustees, parents and students. These forums provided EQAO with information about the assessments and their administration in schools, the value/usefulness of the various EQAO reports for accountability and improvement planning and the importance of the professional development/teacher training aspect of EQAO's work. EQAO also sought public comment on the final report of the external evaluation of the agency's assessment program (Education Quality and Accountability Office, 2004).

ANALYSIS AND SYNTHESIS

EQAO considered all of the information obtained from both the internal and external review processes and paid particular attention to the feasibility of the various assessment design options presented in the OISE/UT final report. These design options were considered in light of

- the research on best practices in "exemplary" assessment programs;
- key areas and needs identified through the consultation process with stakeholders;
- the impact on schools and school boards in terms of streamlining and simplifying administrative procedures to decrease the workload of staff and limit the amount of disruption in classrooms and
- the impact on EQAO with regard to timing, human resources and costs.

The results of this evaluation confirmed for EQAO that many of its assessment practices were best-of-class. The recommendations, information and insights received through the review also suggested some areas where enhancements could be made. Implementation of these refinements began with the 2004-2005 assessments (Education Quality and Accountability Office, 2004).

SUMMARY

The Ensuring Quality Assessments review was an appraisal evaluation which involved a team of external experts who examined EQAO's assessment processes and made recommendations for program refinement. The review also included an internal evaluation component, in which EQAO staff contributed by conducting jurisdictional research and facilitating stakeholder consultations. Involving EQAO personnel in the process was important for several reasons. The agency was in its formative years, and many staff members were relatively new to the field of large-scale assessment. The interactions between staff and the external experts provided a unique professional development opportunity. Furthermore, the jurisdictional review not only provided EQAO with important information for the review, but it also meant that staff members were positioned to reflect on the agency's processes in light of other best practices: In a sense, they were conducting a form of self-evaluation.

The evaluation reflected many of the principles of best practice identified in *The Program Evaluation Standards* and the *Guiding Principles for Evaluators.*

- The study of EQAO's assessment processes was conducted by an experienced team of assessment and measurement experts in conjunction with several Canadian and American technical advisors.

- The study design, which included analysis of EQAO assessment-related materials, documentation and data, as well as jurisdictional reviews and consultations, generated sufficient information on which to address the evaluation's purpose, topics of interest and research questions.

- Communication was a key element of the study and was important in many ways. The principal investigators of the external team met on many occasions with EQAO senior management to establish a clear, mutual understanding of the study's purposes and parameters and to provide progress briefings. An OISE/UT professor was named as the university's liaison with EQAO's Chief Executive Officer to ensure ongoing communication and collaboration between the two organizations. Communication with all stakeholder groups, before the project began, during the consultation process and following submission of the external team's final report ensured all interested parties received the information they needed, and there were no misunderstandings or surprises.

- During the consultation process, the positions/comments of all participants/stakeholder groups were noted, summarized and distributed back to them to ensure all positions were accurately captured. Individual feedback was kept confidential; comments were aggregated at the group level (e.g., Assessment Advisory Committee, Catholic Principals' Council of Ontario, Ontario Public School Boards' Association, Ontario Secondary School Teachers' Federation, Ontario Parent Council, Minister's Advisory Council on Special Education).

BRITISH COLUMBIA

ACCREDITATION

ACCREDITATION
Accreditation of Maple Ridge Secondary School

14

BACKGROUND AND CONTEXT OF THE STUDY

Maple Ridge Secondary School

Maple Ridge Secondary School (part of British Columbia's School District 42, Maple Ridge-Pitt Meadows) was a public high school in the city of Maple Ridge, located in the northeastern section of Metropolitan Vancouver in the province's Lower Mainland (see Figure 10). In 1988, when this study was conducted, Maple Ridge had a population of approximately 52,000, and the school comprised about 900 students and 80 staff members.

Figure 10 | Location of Maple Ridge in the Metropolitan Vancouver Area

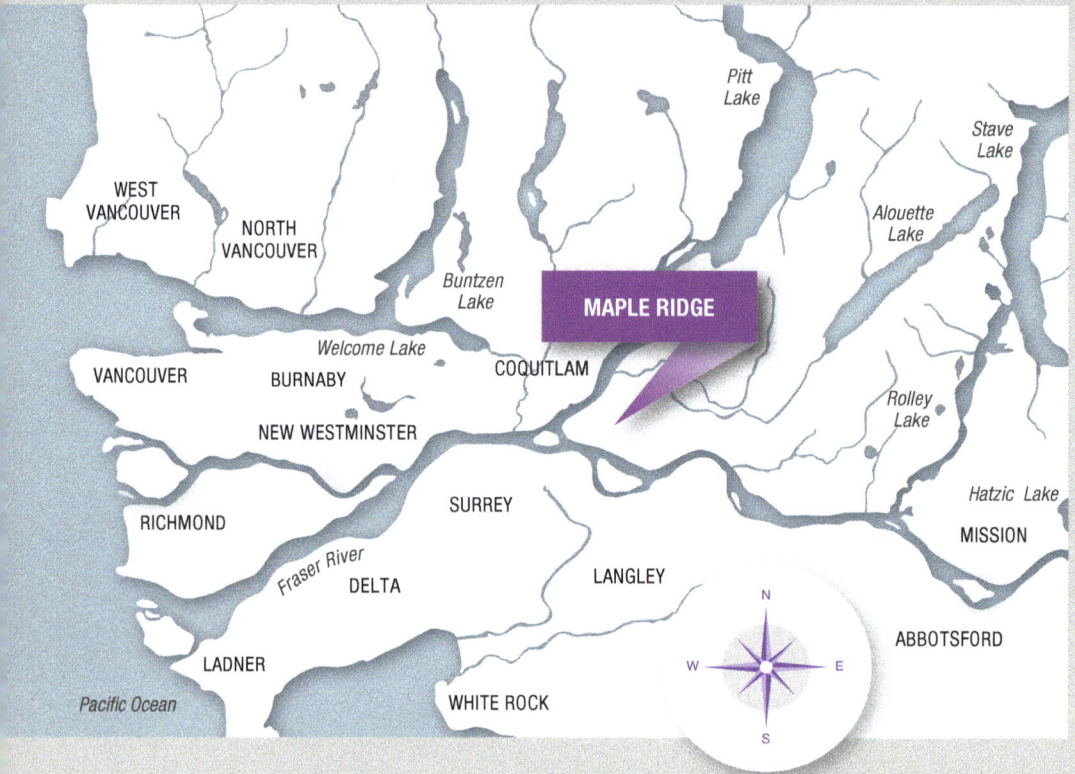

School Accreditation Program

According to Hodgkinson (1995), the school accreditation program was one of seven elements of the British Columbia education system's accountability framework (others included Ministry and school board annual reports, large-scale assessments of student achievement, program evaluations and education indicators projects). School accreditation was first introduced into the province in the 1920s and had a secondary-school focus. Initially, inspectors visited schools to determine whether they were competent to set their own final examinations for students in Grades 8 to 12. Independent reports were filed by the inspector and school principal with the Ministry of Education. Over the years, the accreditation program evolved from an inspectorial function, based on external evaluation, to a model incorporating internal and external evaluation components with a focus on school improvement and the development of a school growth plan. Prior to the 1988-1989 school year, only secondary schools were expected to participate in the accreditation process. Beginning with the 1988-1989 school year, however, a small number of elementary schools participated on a voluntary basis, and eventually the program became mandatory for all elementary and secondary schools in the province.

Accreditation followed a six-year cycle in which a school receiving full accreditation would need to go through the process every six years.[1]

PURPOSE OF THE STUDY

In the new model, the purpose of accreditation was to improve the quality of schools by ensuring that they demonstrated provincial education standards with respect to the three goals of education: intellectual, human and social, and career development and the five attributes of the public school system: accessibility, relevance, equity, quality and accountability and by ensuring that schools reflected on their performance and developed suitable improvement/growth plans. The external evaluation was meant to gather information and report on the school's performance with regard to the provincial education standards and the adequacy of the school's improvement/growth plan.

---

[1] British Columbia's school accreditation program was discontinued following a review of the program that was conducted in 1999.

THE STUDY TEAM

According to Wallbank-Macfarlane-Tindall (1999), external evaluation teams were made up of a minimum of three members with relevant expertise who were approved by the Minister of Education. The external team comprised parents, teachers, administrators, district office staff, students and community members as appropriate. Members of the external team were expected to be from other school districts and not from the district in which the school to be accredited was located. A registry of potential external team chairs and members was maintained by an organization called Accreditation Services (under the supervision of the Ministry), which coordinated the selection of external team members and provided training for those who had not previously participated on an external evaluation team. The chair of the external team was selected by the school district in consultation with the Ministry.

For the accreditation of Maple Ridge Secondary School, the chair of the external team was a former Superintendent of Schools (called a Director of Education in some jurisdictions), and the team members included a principal, a former Modern Languages Department head, a mathematics and science teacher and a parent. Three of the members had served on external accreditation teams in the past.

EVALUATION METHODOLOGY

Ministry-Mandated Process

The accreditation process required that during the accreditation year, schools collect data on Ministry-mandated topics and develop an internal report, including a school growth/improvement plan, according to criteria established by the Ministry. An internal school team (made up of teachers, non-teaching staff, parents and students) conducting a self-evaluation with reference to a set of 33 topics and standard procedures developed by the Ministry and followed by all schools. The accreditation topics were as follows (Cabatoff, 2001):

1 | Students' ability to access, evaluate and use information

2 | Students' ability to express themselves effectively through writing, speech and a variety of other forms of representing

3 | Students' ability to analyze critically, reason and think independently, solve problems and make decisions

4 | Students' ability to think creatively and express themselves creatively

5 | Students' co-operative and team skills

6 | Students' ability to set goals and work toward attainment of their educational, training and career objectives

7 | Students' knowledge, skills and attitudes necessary for employment and future education

8 | Students' awareness of the value of lifelong learning

9 | Students' sense of self-confidence and personal initiative

10 | Students' sense of social responsibility

11 | Students' tolerance and respect for the ideas and beliefs of others

12 | Students' knowledge, skills and attitudes related to the language arts curriculum

13 | Students' knowledge, skills and attitudes related to the social studies curriculum

14 | Students' knowledge, skills and attitudes related to the science curriculum

15 | Students' knowledge, skills and attitudes related to the mathematics curriculum

16 | Students' knowledge, skills and attitudes related to the physical education curriculum

17 | Students' knowledge, skills and attitudes related to the fine arts (drama, art, music and dance) curriculum

18 | Students' knowledge, skills and attitudes related to the applied skills (technology education, business education and home economics) curriculum

19 | Students' knowledge, skills and attitudes related to the personal planning/career and personal planning curriculum

20 | Students' knowledge, skills and attitudes related to information and computer technology

21 | School's provision for students' active participation in learning

22 | School's provision for students' learning occurring in a variety of ways

23 | School's provision for students' learning occurring at different rates

24 | School's provision for students' learning occurring both individually and co-operatively in groups

25 | School's provision of effective student evaluation and reporting strategies

26 | School's provision of a safe and accessible learning environment for all students

27 | School's provision of programs and services to meet the needs of all students

28 | School's provision of programs and activities that are relevant to all students

29 | School's provision for regular monitoring of student, parent and community satisfaction

30 | School's provision for parents and community representatives being regularly informed of the progress of school improvement and being involved as partners in planning

31 | School's fair allocation of human and material resources

32 | Staff working both independently and collegially to examine and improve their practice

33 | Students', parents' and staff leadership

In developing its report, the internal team assessed the school's and students' performance through the examination of each of the accreditation topics with respect to opportunities provided (what the school was doing to provide a quality education for all students) and performance indicators (information that demonstrated the level of school and student performance). To gather data for this self-assessment process, the internal team administered surveys to school staff, students, parents and other members of the school community and also gathered a range of student performance indicators (e.g., teacher-administered test results and student performance on provincial learning assessments conducted by the Ministry). The Ministry provided schools with survey protocols and a "Record of Evidence" form to assist them in gathering, recording and analyzing data and information to inform decision-making regarding school improvement/ the school growth plan.

According to Wallbank-Macfarlane-Tindall (1999), the internal report was expected to include the following components:

- List of participants
- Summary of procedures
- Statement of the inclusiveness of the process (stakeholder involvement)
- School and community context
- School's mission statement
- Completed "Record of Evidence" forms for each of the 33 accreditation topics
- Any other topics and associated evidence or documentation identified by the school
- Draft school growth/improvement plan, including a long-term overview
- Plan for demonstrating regular communication and reporting to stakeholders/partners

Following the school's self-assessment process, an external team from outside the school district visited the school and conducted a review over a three- to five-day period. Prior to the visit, the external team reviewed the school's internal report and improvement/growth plan. The external team's primary roles were to:

- validate the internal report, including the appropriateness of the evidence of success provided for each of the accreditation topics;
- assess the level of stakeholder involvement in the school's ongoing self-assessment process;

- evaluate the appropriateness of the school growth/improvement plan and

- make a recommendation on accreditation status.

During its visit, the team conducted a variety of activities, including

- meeting school personnel and students;

- conducting interviews (using standard protocols) with administrators, teachers, non-teaching staff, students, parents and other community members;

- observing instruction in classrooms;

- reviewing the evidence as provided in the internal report and comparing it with what was observed/learned on-site and

- writing the external evaluation report.

The external team began drafting its report from the first day of the visit, and as the week progressed, the report was revised to reflect new information. At the end of the visit, the external team presented its draft findings to the internal team and principal or the entire school staff (depending on the needs of the school/school board) for information and reaction. Any comments from the school and/or school board were considered in preparing the final version of the report. The final report was presented to the school, school board and Ministry of Education within two weeks of the school visit. Based on its evaluation, the external team recommended to the Ministry that accreditation should be awarded to or withheld from the given school. In cases where accreditation was denied, the school district Superintendent of Schools was expected to prepare a strategy to address the issues identified in the external report, and the process of self- and external assessment was repeated the following year.

Maple Ridge Secondary School Accreditation Process

Data-Gathering Methods

In the case of the Maple Ridge Secondary School accreditation, over the course of two school years the members of the internal team used professional development days to conduct accreditation-related activities and develop a comprehensive report. The external team had received copies of the internal report for review and reference prior to the school visit.

On the Sunday afternoon prior to the external team's visit, the team's chair met with the school's principal and vice-principal and school board officials to discuss the review process, which in this instance took place over a five-day period (Monday to Friday). The internal team members did not meet the external team until they arrived at the school for the visit. On Sunday evening, the members of the external team met privately for a planning session, and each had specific roles to play. Individual members were assigned to observe classes/instruction in given departments as follows:

- Modern Languages and Social Studies Departments
- English Language and Literature Departments
- Mathematics and Science Departments
- Fine Arts and Home Economics Departments
- Physical Education and Business Education Departments

One member of the team (the individual who was a Superintendent of Schools) assumed the additional task of interviewing school and school board administrators.

During the course of the week, external team members interviewed random samples of 20 school staff (i.e., teachers and non-teaching staff), 20 students (four from each grade), 10 parents and five local merchants, with reference to the mandated accreditation topics.

All external team members were expected to arrive early at the school each day to observe life in the hallways, playgrounds, school office and classrooms. On the Monday morning, the external team members met with the whole school at an assembly, where they were introduced to the students and staff, and the external team described the purpose of the visit and the process that would be followed.

DATA/INFORMATION ANALYSIS AND REPORTING

In the days that followed, the external team members attended to their specific tasks of making observations and interviewing in the school and community. Concurrent with this work, the external team also drafted its report. Each evening, the team members met to share their observations, compare them with the findings/statements in the internal report (including the school growth plan) and draft/revise the external report accordingly. On the fifth and last day of its visit (Friday), the external team verbally presented its findings to the school staff, provided the school and school board with a draft report and invited comments. One week after the visit, the external team received comments from the school and board, made revisions to the report as appropriate and two weeks following the school visit sent the final version of the report to the school, school board and Ministry of Education.

SUMMARY

The purpose of Maple Ridge Secondary School's accreditation study was to gather information and report on the school's performance with regard to the provincial education standards and the adequacy of the school's improvement/growth plan. The evaluation was successful in that

- the external review was conducted in accordance with established Ministry policies and guidelines, and the Ministry-mandated methodology produced a report that met the provincial requirement;

- the Ministry, school board and school ensured that the internal team received the training, as well as standard guidelines and materials, to assist it to conduct the accreditation activities and develop the internal report;

- prior to the external team's visit to the school, the Ministry (Accreditation Services) provided training to the two individuals who had not previously served on an external evaluation team;

- appropriate communication with stakeholders occurred through the required school assemblies, staff meetings, consultation with partner community groups and reports;

- all data/information was aggregated at the group/school levels to ensure anonymity and confidentiality regarding individuals' information and

- reports were prepared and distributed in a timely fashion and in accordance with Ministry guidelines.

CONCLUSION

Over the years, I have been associated with a great many program evaluation projects, only a sub-set of which is presented in this book. Every evaluation was successful in that the methodology used generated the data/information necessary to answer the given research questions/topics of focus, and the clients were pleased with the approaches used and the final reports. There are several reasons for this success, including the following elements of effective evaluation planning and implementation:

Acquire a clear understanding of the program and its context, the object of the evaluation, as well as the study's purposes and expectations from the outset. These form the foundation upon which the study design is built and may inform the evaluators as to whether or not they wish to become involved in the study. (I have declined to participate in an evaluation when, in my judgement, the project was politically motivated, and it was evident the prospective client had a predetermined outcome in mind.)

Establish a good working relationship with the client and stakeholders. The evaluator should take time to learn as much as possible about the requirements of the evaluation, including whether or not stakeholders will participate, and if so, what their role(s) will be. If stakeholders have a role(s) to play, opportunities for information sharing will bring an air of transparency, respect and trust to the project. Being attentive to stakeholder needs (where appropriate) goes a long way toward obtaining buy-in from everyone with an interest in the study.

Focus the evaluation on reasonable objects or aspects of the program to be examined. If time is not taken to determine the key aspects of focus at the outset, the project runs the risk of becoming too broad and therefore unmanageable.

Assemble a study team that is capable of delivering a quality result. When responding to a Request for Proposals or when consulting with a prospective client, give careful attention to the likely knowledge, skills and experience the project will require.

Give careful attention to all aspects of study design. Once the evaluation's purposes, issues and research questions/topics of focus are identified, consider all possible sources of data and information and data- and information-collection methods, and select those that will most reliably and efficiently generate the required data/information. Develop a complete work plan, including the reporting scheme consistent with the agreed-upon schedule. It is important that the plan for disseminating results to the various audiences be established early on.

Incorporate the standards of best practice and ethical principles into the evaluation. Consider how *The Program Evaluation Standards* and *Guiding Principles for Evaluators* can be built into each stage of the program evaluation.

Communicate! Communicate! Communicate! Effective communication has been fundamental to the success of every evaluation project in which I have participated. Evaluators must appreciate that the time taken (for example) to consult with clients at the outset and throughout the life of a project, to provide regular briefings/progress reports and to interact with stakeholders is time well spent. Including a well-conceived communication strategy as part of the overall work plan will mitigate against unnecessary (and sometimes embarrassing and/or costly) misunderstandings and surprises.

REFERENCES

Alkin, M. (1972). *A Classification Scheme for Objectives-based Evaluation Systems.* (CSE Report No. 79). Los Angeles, CA: Centre for the Study of Evaluation.

American Educational Research Association, American Psychological Association, & National Council on Measurement in Education. (2014). *Standards for Educational and Psychological Testing.* Washington, DC: American Educational Research Association.

American Evaluation Association. (2004). *Guiding Principles for Evaluators.* Fairhaven, MA: Author. Retrieved January 22, 2009 from http://www.eval.org/p/cm/ld/fid=51.

Axinn, W. G., & Pearce, L. D. (2006). *Mixed Method Data Collection Strategies.* Cambridge, UK: Cambridge University Press.

Cabatoff, K. (2001). The Long March from Evaluation to Accreditation: Québec's New "Government Management Framework." *The Canadian Journal of Program Evaluation,* (Special Issue), pp. 73-88.

Christie, C., & Alkin, M. (2004). Objectives Based Evaluation. In Mathison, S. (Ed.), *Encyclopedia of Evaluation.* Thousand Oaks, CA: Sage Publications, Inc.

Coleman, J. S., Campbell, E. Q., Hobson, C. J., McPartland, J., Mood, A. M., Weinfeld, F. D., & York, R. L. (1966). *Equality of Educational Opportunity.* Washington, DC: U.S. Government Printing Office.

Council for National Academic Awards. (1990). *Accreditation: The American Experience.* London: Author.

Daniel, C. A. (2012). *Reader-Friendly Reports: A No-Nonsense Guide to Effective Writing for MBAs, Consultants, and Other Professionals.* Columbus, OH: McGraw-Hill Education.

Deal, T. E., & Kennedy, A. A. (1982). *Corporate Cultures.* Reading, MA: Addison-Wesley.

Earl, L. M. (1995). Assessment and Accountability in Education in Ontario. *Canadian Journal of Education,* 20 (1), pp. 45-55.

Education Quality and Accountability Office. (2004). *Ensuring Quality Assessments: Enhancements to EQAO's Assessment Program, The Move Forward.* Toronto, ON: Queen's Printer for Ontario.

Eisner, E. W. (1985a). *The Educational Imagination (2nd ed.).* New York: Macmillan Publishing, Inc.

Eisner, E. W. (1985b). Educational connoisseurship and criticism. In Madaus, G.F., Kellaghan, T., & Stufflebeam, D.L. (Eds.), *Evaluation Models.* Boston, MA: Kluwer-Nijhoff Publishing, pp. 335-348.

Eisner, E. W. (1994). *The Educational Imagination: On the Design and Evaluation of School Programs (3rd ed.).* New York: Macmillan Publishing, Inc.

Fitzpatrick, J. L., Sanders, J. R., & Worthen, B. R. (2011). *Program Evaluation: Alternative Approaches and Practical Guidelines.* Upper Saddle River, NJ: Pearson Education, Inc.

Fretwell, D. (2003). A framework for evaluating vocational education and training (VET). *European Journal of Education,* 38 (2), pp. 177-190.

Gottman, J. N., & Clasen, R. E. (1972). *Evaluation in Education: A Practitioner's Guide.* Itasca, IL: F. E. Peacock Publishers, Inc.

Gupta, K. (1999). *A Practical Guide to Needs Assessment.* San Francisco, CA: Jossy-Bass/Pfeiffer.

Hodgkinson, C. (1978). *Towards a Philosophy of Administration.* Oxford: Basil Blackwell.

Hodgkinson, D. (1995). Accountability in Education in British Columbia. *Canadian Journal of Education,* 20 (1), pp. 18-26.

Hofstrand, D., & Holz-Clause, M. (2009). *What is a Feasibility Study?* Ames, IA: Ag Decision Maker, Department of Economics, University Extension, Iowa State University. Retrieved November 16, 2014 from http://www.extension.iastate.edu/ agdm/wholefarm/html/c5-65.html.

Holden, D. J., & Zimmerman, M. A. (Eds.). (2009). *A Practical Guide to Program Evaluation Planning: Theory and Case Examples.* Thousand Oaks, CA: Sage Publications, Ltd.

Hudson, J., Mayne, J., & Thomlison, R. (1992). *Action-Oriented Evaluation in Organizations: Canadian Practices.* Toronto, ON: Wall & Emerson, Inc.

Jencks, C., Smith, M., Acland, H., Bane, M. J., Cohen, D., Gintis, H., Heyns, B., & Michelson, S. (1973). *Inequality: A Reassessment of the Effect of Family and Schooling in America.* New York: Basic Books.

Joint Committee on Standards for Educational Evaluation. (2011). *The Program Evaluation Standards (3rd ed.).* Thousand Oaks, CA: Sage Publications, Ltd. Standards statements retrieved October 18, 2014 from http://www.jcsee.org/program-evaluation-standards-statements.

Johnston, J. H. (1987). Values, culture, and the effective school. *NASSP Bulletin,* 71 (497), pp. 79-88.

Jones, R. M. (1991). *Organizational Culture of Three High Performance Secondary Schools in British Columbia.* Victoria, BC: Doctoral dissertation, University of Victoria.

Jones, R. M. (1998). Evaluating the Ontario Academic Course Teacher In-service Program. *The Canadian Journal of Program Evaluation,* 13 (2), pp. 113-122.

Jones, R. M. (2003). Canada - The School Sector. In *Educational Evaluation around the World.* Copenhagen, DK: The Danish Evaluation Institute, pp. 43-51.

Kozma, R. B., (Ed.) (2003). *Technology, Innovation, and Educational Change: A Global Perspective.* A Report of the Second Information Technology in Education Study, Module 2. Eugene, OR: International Society for Technology in Education (ISTE).

Legislative Assembly of Ontario. (1996). *Education Quality and Accountability Office Act.* Retrieved December 27, 2014 from http://www.e-laws.gov.on.ca/html/ statutes/english/elaws_statutes_96e11_e.htm.

Lincoln, Y. S., & Guba, E. G. (1985). *Naturalistic Inquiry.* Beverly Hills, CA: Sage Publications, Inc.

Love, A. J. (1991). *Internal Evaluation: Building Organizations from Within.* Newbury Park, CA: Sage Publications, Inc.

MacDonald, B., & Walker, R. (1977). Case-study and the social philosophy of educational research. In Hamilton, D., MacDonald, B., King, C., Jenkins, D., & Parlett, M. (Eds.), *Beyond the Numbers Game.* London: Macmillan Education.

Mathison, S. (Ed.) (2005). *Encyclopedia of Evaluation.* Thousand Oaks, CA: Sage Publications, Inc.

Maxwell, T. W. (1996). Accountability: The case of accreditation of British Columbia's public schools. *Canadian Journal of Education,* 21 (1), pp. 18-34. Retrieved February 27, 2009 from http://www.csse.ca/CJE/Articles/FullText/CJE21-1-03Maxwell.pdf.

McCawley, P. F. (2009). *Methods for Conducting an Educational Needs Assessment: Guidelines for Cooperative Extension System Professionals.* University of Idaho Extension. Retrieved October 18, 2014 from http://www.cals.uidaho.edu/edcomm/pdf/bul/bul0870.pdf.

McNamara, C. (2008a). *Basic Guide to Program Evaluation.* Retrieved November 26, 2008 from http://www.managementhelp.org/evaluatn/fnl_eval.htm.

McNamara, C. (2008b). *Basics of Developing Case Studies.* Retrieved March 15, 2009 from http://managementhelp.org/evaluatn/casestdy.htm.

Metz, H. C. (Ed.) (1993). *Saudi Arabia: A Country Study (5th ed.).* Washington, DC: Federal Research Division, Library of Congress. Retrieved September 22, 2014 from https://archive.org/stream/saudiarabiacount00metz_0/saudiarabiacount-00metz_0_djvu.txt.

Miles, M. B., & Huberman, A. M. (2013). *Qualitative Data Analysis: A Methods Sourcebook (3rd ed.).* Thousand Oaks, CA: Sage Publications, Inc.

National Study of School Evaluation. (1979). *Evaluation Criteria (5th ed.).* Washington, DC: Author.

Netzley, M., & Snow, C. (2001). *Guide to Report Writing (Guide to Business Communication Series)*. Upper Saddle River, NJ: Prentice Hall, Inc.

Olsen, W. (2012). *Data Collection: Key Debates and Methods in Social Research*. Thousand Oaks, CA: Sage Publications, Inc.

Ott, R. L., & Longnecker, M. T. (2008). *An Introduction to Statistical Methods and Data Analysis (6th ed.)*. Stamford, CT: Cengage Learning, Inc.

Ouchi, W. G. (1981). *Theory Z*. Reading, MA: Addison-Wesley.

Owen, J. M. (2007). *Program Evaluation: Forms and Approaches (3rd ed.)*. New York, NY: The Guilford Press.

Owens, T. R. (1973). Educational evaluation by adversary proceedings. In House, E. R. (Ed.), *School Evaluation: The Politics and Process*. Berkeley, CA: McCutchan Publishing.

Peck, R., Olsen, C., & Devore, J. L. (2011). *Introduction to Statistics and Data Analysis (4th ed.)*. Pacific Grove, CA: Brooks/Cole Publishing Co.

Pelgrum, W., & Anderson, R. (1999). *ICT and the Emerging Paradigm for Lifelong Learning*. Amsterdam, NL: International Association for the Evaluation of Educational Achievement.

Peters, T. J., & Waterman, R. H. (1982). *In Search of Excellence*. New York: Harper & Row.

Popham, W. J., & Carlson, D. (1983). Deep dark deficits of the adversary evaluation model. In Madaus, G. F., Scriven, M., & Stufflebeam, D. L. (Eds.), *Evaluation Models*. Boston: Kluwer-Nijhoff, pp. 205-214.

Principles for Fair Student Assessment Practices for Education in Canada. (1993). Edmonton, AB: Joint Advisory Committee. Retrieved December 21, 2013, from http://www2.education.ualberta.ca/educ/psych/crame/files/eng_prin.pdf.

Provus, M. (1971). *Discrepancy Evaluation*. Berkeley, CA: McCutcheon Publishing.

Riordan, D. G. (2013). *Technical Report Writing Today (10th ed.)*. Stamford, CT: Cengage Learning, Inc.

Rippey, R. M. (Ed.). (1975). *Studies in Transactional Evaluation.* Berkeley, CA: McCutchan Publishing.

Royal Commission on Learning. (1994). *For the Love of Learning: Report of the Royal Commission on Learning (Short Version).* Toronto, ON: Queen's Printer for Ontario.

Rutter, M., Maugham, B., Mortimore, P., & Ouston, J. (1979). *Fifteen Thousand Hours: Secondary Schools and Their Effects on Children.* Cambridge, MA: Harvard University Press.

Saphier, J., & King, M. (1985). Good seeds grow in strong cultures. *Educational Leadership,* 42 (6), pp. 67-74.

Saskatchewan Education. (1984). *Directions: The Final Report of the Minister's Advisory Committee on Curriculum and Instruction.* Regina, SK: Author.

Saskatchewan Education. (1989). *Saskatchewan School-Based Program Evaluation Resource Book.* Regina, SK: Author.

Scriven, M. (1974). Educational perspectives and procedures. In Popham, W. J. (Ed.), *Evaluation in Education.* Berkeley, CA: McCutchan Publishing Corp., pp. 34-93.

Scriven, M. (1980). *The Logic of Evaluation.* Interness, CA: Edgepress.

Stake, R. E. (1967). The countenance of educational evaluation. *Teachers College Record,* 68 (7), pp. 523-530.

Stake, R. E. (1995). *The Art of Case Study Research.* Thousand Oaks, CA: Sage Publications, Inc.

Stenzel, N. (1976). *Adversary Processes and Their Potential Use in Evaluation for the Illinois Office of Education.* Springfield, IL: Illinois Department of Education.

Stevens, R. E. (1982). *How to Prepare a Feasibility Study: A Step-by-Step Guide Including 3 Model Studies.* Englewood Cliffs, NJ: Prentice-Hall.

Stevens, R. E., Loudon, D. L., Sherwood, P. K., & Dunn, J. P. (2006). *Market Opportunity Analysis: Text and Cases.* NY: Routledge.

Stufflebeam, D. L. (1985). *Conducting Educational Needs Assessments.* Boston, MA: Kluwer-Nijhoff Publishing.

Stufflebeam, D. L. (1994). Empowerment evaluation, objectivist evaluation, and evaluation standards: Where the future of evaluation should not go and where it needs to go. *Evaluation Practice,* 15, pp. 321-338.

Stufflebeam, D. L. (2000). The CIPP model for evaluation. In Stufflebeam, D. L., Madaus, G. F., & Kellaghan, T. (Eds.), *Evaluation Models (2nd ed.).* Boston: Kluwer Academic Publishers, pp. 279-317.

Stufflebeam, D. L., & Coryn, C. L. S. (2014). *Evaluation Theory, Models, & Applications.* San Francisco, CA: Jossey-Bass.

Stufflebeam, D. L., McCormick, C. H., Brinkerhoff, R. O., & Nelson, C. O. (1985). *Conducting Educational Needs Assessments.* Boston, MA: Kluwer-Nijhoff Publishing.

Stufflebeam, D. L., & Shinkfield, A. J. (1985). *Systematic Evaluation.* Boston, MA: Kluwer-Nijhoff Publishing.

Stufflebeam, D. L., & Webster, W. J. (1988). Evaluation as an administrative function. In Boyan, N. (Ed.), *Handbook of Research on Educational Administration.* White Plains, NY: Longman.

Tyler, R. (1942). General statement on evaluation. *Journal of Educational Research,* 35, pp. 492-501.

United Nations Economic and Social Commission for Western Asia. (2010). *The Demographic Profile of Saudi Arabia.* Beirut, Lebanon: United Nations. Retrieved October 5, 2014 from http://www.escwa.un.org/popin/members/SaudiArabia.pdf.

University of Wisconsin Center for Cooperatives. (1998). *Conducting a Feasibility Study.* Madison, WI: Author. Retrieved November 20, 2014 from http://www.uwcc.wisc.edu/manual/chap_5.html.

Van Sant O'Neill, D., Cohen, S., Hadikin, B., Koretchuk, P., Price, D., & Swenson, S. (1988). *Research Backgrounder on School Culture.* Victoria, BC: Ministry of Education, Province of British Columbia.

Wallbank-Macfarlane-Tindall. (1999). *Evaluation: School Accreditation Program Phase 2.* Report prepared for the British Columbia Ministry of Education, August 27, 1999.

Watkins, R., West Meiers, M., & Visser, Y. (2012). *A Guide to Assessing Needs: Essential Tools for Collecting Information, Making Decisions, and Achieving Development Results.* (World Bank Training Services). World Bank Publications.

Weller, S. C., & Romney, A. K. (1988). *Systematic Data Collection (Qualitative Research Methods Series 10).* Thousand Oaks, CA: Sage Publications, Inc.

Witkin, B. R., & Altschuld, J. W. (1995). *Planning and Conducting Needs Assessments: A Practical Guide.* Thousand Oaks, CA: Sage Publications, Inc.

Wolf, R. L. (1975). Trial by jury. A new evaluation method. *Phi Delta Kappan,* 57 (3), pp. 185-187.

Wolfe, R., Childs, R., & Elgie, S. (2004). *Final Report of the External Evaluation of EQAO's Assessment Processes.* Report prepared for the Education Quality and Accountability Office. Ontario Institute for Studies in Education of the University of Toronto.

Worthen, B. R., Borg, W. R., & White, K. R. (1993). *Measurement and Evaluation in the Schools.* White Plains, NY: Longman Publishing Group.

Worthen, B. R., Sanders, J. R., & Fitzpatrick, J. L. (1997). *Program Evaluation: Alternative Approaches and Practical Guidelines (2nd ed.).* White Plains, NY: Addison Wesley Longman, Inc.

Yarbrough, D. B., Shulha, L. M., Hopson, R. K., & Caruthers, F. A. (2011). *The Program Evaluation Standards: A Guide for Evaluators and Evaluation Users.* Thousand Oaks, CA: Sage Publications, Ltd.

Yin, R. K. (2013). *Case Study Research: Design and Methods (Applied Social Research Methods).* Thousand Oaks, CA: Sage Publications, Inc.